MAX WEBER'S INSIGHTS AND ERRORS

D1453719

MAX WEBER'S INSIGHTS AND ERRORS

STANISLAV ANDRESKI

Routledge
Taylor & Francis Group

LONDON AND NEW YORK

First published in 1984

Reprinted in 2006 by
Routledge
2 Park Square, Milton Park, Abingdon, Oxfordshire, OX14 4RN
270 Madison Avenue, New York NY 10016
Routledge is an imprint of the Taylor & Francis Group

First issued in paperback 2010

British Library Cataloguing in Publication Data
A CIP catalogue record for this book
is available from the British Library

Max Weber's Insights and Errors

ISBN 978-0-415-40210-1 (set)
ISBN 978-0-415-540216-3 (volume)(hbk)
ISBN 978-0-415-61107-7 (volume)(pbk)

Routledge Library Editions: Weber

Max Weber's insights and errors

Stanislav Andreski

Professor of Sociology, University of Reading

LONDON AND NEW YORK

First published in 1984
by Routledge
2 Park Square, Milton Park, Abingdon, Oxon, OX14 4RN
270 Madison Ave, New York NY 10016

Set in 10/11pt Times
by Columns of Reading

Library of Congress Cataloging in Publication Data

Andreski, Stanislav.

Max Weber's insights and errors.
(International library of sociology)
Includes index.
1. Weber, Max, 1864-1920. 2. Sociology. I. Title.
II. Series.
HM22.G3W3975   1984   301'.092'4   83-26974

British Library CIP data available

ISBN 0-7102-0051-X

Contents

Preface

When nearly four decades ago I took an optional paper in Theories and Methods of Sociology, as a part of a degree in economics in the University of London, Max Weber was not included in the syllabus. Morris Ginsberg (then the sole professor of sociology in Britain) did not say much about him. Our main textbook – Sorokin's *Contemporary Sociological Theories* (still well worth reading for other reasons) – discussed Weber briefly on a par with dozens, if not hundreds, of other writers. At that time only two pieces of Weber's writings were available in English: *The Protestant Ethic and the Spirit of Capitalism* and *General Economic History*. As the latter was on the reading list of the course in Economic History 1760–1914, I read it and was entranced with the last three chapters. They seemed to me to explain what the other books on the reading list merely described. When I asked Ginsberg about Weber he said he was well worth reading but he gave me the impression that he was not as good as L.T. Hobhouse – Ginsberg's teacher and predecessor who certainly was a scholar of high quality and is still well worth reading, but no great innovator. However, after Karl Mannheim (who as an exile had to be contented with a lectureship) told me that Weber was the greatest writer on sociology, and that one cannot become a competent sociologist without reading his main works, I decided to brush up my German specifically for this purpose. I had more opportunities to do so later, during my service with the occupation forces in Germany: I managed to obtain, after a long search, all the books in exchange for food or cigarettes. When I found *Wirtschaft und Gesellschaft* I could hardly sleep with excitement. It was the first book in German which I had read from cover to cover, and (while waiting for demobilisation) I spent eight months doing nothing else but deciphering it laboriously with the aid of a dictionary. By the time I got to the end, I could read anything in German with ease.

I became an admirer of Weber (and of a number of other German writers of his era) when I still had fresh in the mind various memories which could well have prejudiced me against everything made in Germany, especially by outspoken national-ists. None the less, in my first book I called him 'the greatest thinker to whom the name of sociologist can be applied'. I have even made a very illustrious convert to the circle of British admirers of Weber, which at that time was exceedingly small: namely, the co-founder of the functionalist school of anthro-pology Radcliffe-Brown. After retiring from his chair at Oxford he came as a visiting professor to Rhodes University College, South Africa, where I was a junior lecturer; and, despite the difference of age, I became his closest friend there. In our many chats I often spoke about Weber and lent him my copy of *Wirtschaft und Gesellschaft*. Having read some of it, he said to me: 'it is really damned good stuff. . . . What a pity nobody told me about him earlier.'

I mention these autobiographical details to make clear that it is not my purpose to debunk Weber. Whenever I re-read him it gives me great pleasure to savour the fertility and range of his intellect. None the less, you cannot build anything deserving the name of science (even in the loosest sense of this word) on ancestor worship. Weber himself said: 'we work in order to be overtaken'. It is one of the aspects of the sad state of the social sciences that we have an incessant flood of 'isms', and the famous figures of the past are treated as idols either to be worshipped or pulled down and dumped on a scrap heap. Often adoration goes together with scant comprehension of what the old master was getting at, which is especially easy if he writes in a manner undistinguished by clarity. It is easier to go on repeating a few neologisms and quotations than to try to go farther along the paths which a great thinker has opened. It is not surprising, therefore, that Weber has become something of a totem, often invoked to give an air of scholarly respectability to writings which sin gravely against all the ideals of scholarship which he held. This is connected with the misconceptions widely diffused by some of the most influential commentators (above all Talcott Parsons), who focus on the superficial, often purely verbal points, and fail to appreciate wherein Weber's true greatness lies. My purpose here is to rectify such errors and to put Weber in the correct perspective which would enable more people to treat him as a source of inspiration for inquiries rather than an object of scholasticist genuflexions.

1 Preliminaries

1.1 The personal and political background

The clustering of geniuses in time and space is often cited as evidence of their dependence on the social environment, as there is no reason to suppose that the frequency of births of individuals with extraordinary abilities varies greatly in large populations. Weber's case corroborates this view: his life (1864–1920) falls squarely within the period of intellectual pre-eminence of the German culture which began around the middle of the nineteenth century and ended abruptly with the assumption of power by Adolf Hitler. Weber was a near contemporary of Freud and Max Planck, while Einstein (though a good deal younger) was already recognised as a great man when Weber died. Among his contemporaries doing similar work in Germany there were at least three whose contributions to knowledge are almost as important as his: Karl Kautsky, Otto Hintze and Werner Sombart. Many other excellent scholars helped to win for Germany (or rather for people of German language and culture) a clear pre-eminence in social and historical studies with the exception of economic theory. Though not free from the common shortcomings of German scholarship of his time – such as ponderousness, convoluted style, needless obscurity and the lack of humour – Weber fully embodies its best qualities: the tremendous dedication to the ideals of science, indefatigable industry and boldness in undertaking daunting tasks.

As the offspring of an affluent family, Weber faced no great obstacles in pursuing an academic career, which in those days was very difficult for people of modest means because nobody below the rank of a professor was paid a living wage, many lecturers receiving no payment at all. In a set-up which valued highly hard

1

work and talent Weber advanced rapidly, becoming a professor at thirty. And it must be remembered that at that time this was an elevated position – much higher than what this title means nowadays in Germany or other countries in Europe, not to speak of America. We must not imagine, however, that Weber's influence during his lifetime was commensurate with his present fame: he was unknown in the English-speaking countries, little known on the Continent and (though respected) by no means a dominant figure in Germany. In the survey of sociological theories which was most widely read in the early 1920s (P. Barth, *Philosophie der Geschichte als Soziologie*, 2nd edn, 1922) Max Weber is mentioned nine times – the same number of times as the now almost forgotten Karl Buecher. Friedrich Ratzel and Guillaume de Greef, Emile Durkheim and the now little remembered Frenchman Gabriel Tarde are cited six times. Ferdinand Tönnies and Albert Schaeffle get eleven citations, Karl Kautsky twelve; the now completely forgotten Alois Riehl and the American Franklin Giddings thirteen; Rudolf Stammler and Alfred Fouillé fifteen. The star is Weber's German near contemporary Wilhelm Wundt with forty-two citations – the same number as the by then long-deceased Herbert Spencer.

It is perhaps strange that, despite being civil servants and inclined to show many traits of bureaucratic personality such as an intense pre-occupation with their status, the German professors were less prone than their colleagues elsewhere to attach excessive weight to the boundaries between the disciplines. In Britain law, economics, philosophy and history were studied as watertight compartments, with particularly deleterious effects on the writing of history, which remained very narrow. New subjects, originating on the borders of older disciplines – such as social and economic history or sociology of law – were created in Germany in Weber's lifetime. His own career illustrates the permeability of inter-disciplinary borders in the German universities: he began as a lecturer in law in Berlin, then held chairs of economics at Freiburg and Heidelberg, and eventually became a professor of sociology in Vienna and Munich. His doctoral thesis on the history of the medieval trading companies, as well as his 'Habilitationschrift' (a thesis required for qualifying as a university teacher) on the relationship of the Roman agrarian structure with the law, cut across the division between legal and economic history. His next work – a report on the situation of agricultural labourers in the eastern provinces of the German empire – would nowadays be classified as sociological field-work.

Notwithstanding his extraordinary intellect, in his tastes and values Weber did not diverge from the norm: in politics he was fairly conservative and nationalist. He was also a monarchist, although he thought that Wilhelm II was a vainglorious fool. Weber's moderate conservatism stemmed from scepticism about the chances of great improvements rather than from illusions about the existing state of affairs. As far as his perception of reality is concerned, he can be located neither on the right nor on the left: a rabid marxist could have agreed with what he said at a sociological conference about how the industrialists rule the Saar, while a die-hard conservative could have agreed with what he said about the prospects of socialism. Weber had no vision of a brighter future: he was a pessimist whose goal was to help to avoid disaster. During the war he began to write articles for newspapers and take an active interest in politics, becoming a member of the German delegation negotiating the peace treaty in Versailles. It is doubtful, however, whether he could have been successful as a party politician because he did not mince his words in voicing personal opinions which were too realistic and too bluntly expressed to please the public. Although he did not regard the policies of Germany's rulers as wicked, he made impassioned attacks on them because he thought they were stupid. For instance, like every other nationalist he wished for victory in the war but he thought that the actions of the leaders (especially of the Kaiser) endangered this goal. In contrast to most generals, he was not misled by the smallness of the American army and the lack of militaristic attitudes in the population and recognised the great potential strength of the United States. For this reason he opposed the actions (especially the methods of submarine warfare) which entailed the danger of provoking the entry of the United States into the war against Germany. Had his advice been followed, the First World War might have ended in a truce rather than a defeat for Germany. A quarter of a century earlier he criticised the policy of the German government towards its Polish subjects: again he agreed with its goal of turning these Poles into Germans, but argued that the attempts to suppress Polish language and customs by coercion were counter-productive. His contributions to the debate about a constitution for the new republic after the collapse of the empire were anything but doctrinaire. He favoured a parliamentary constitution on the British lines not because he regarded government by the people as either possible or desirable but because he thought that a powerful parliament would assure a better selection and practical training of political leaders than promotion along the bureaucratic channels, which tends to bring to the helm yes-men incapable of independent judgment.

As his pronouncements concerned the concrete problems of

3

German policy of the time, rather than more general and enduring issues, they are now of only historical interest. He bequeathed neither a programme of social reform nor a statement of political or ethical ideals like, for example, John Stuart Mill's philosophy of liberalism. As far as guidance in any practical action is concerned, the only thing that we can learn from Weber is the hard-headed and deeply probing but not cynical realism which he applied to every question which he discussed.

Weber left neither a school nor even individual disciples who would have continued his work. To a large extent this can be attributed to the complexity and many-sidedness of his thought and the lack of neat and final formulations; which may have been a salutary reaction to the over-simplifications of Comte and Marx but does not alter the fact that we cannot find in Weber's explicit statements the kind of structure which can be discerned in the theories of Marx, Spencer or Freud where we see a few fundamental concepts or assumptions on which the others rest. Despite (or because of) the extraordinary comprehensiveness of his interests, Weber has built no system: he looked at problems from various angles, offering definitions, uncovering causal relations, suggesting explanations or formulating *ad hoc* general-isations on the basis of 'the rule of the thumb' induction. The products were insufficiently co-ordinated to provide a rallying ground for a school. Even in methodology, the value of his contributions lies in the importance of the questions which they raise rather than in the applicability of the answers. The only definite methodological lesson which he has left to posterity is a demonstration of the power of wide-ranging comparative analysis of historical materials. This approach, however, is too difficult to attract many followers, as it requires a confluence of a talent for analysis and theoretical formulation with the taste and capacity for digesting large amounts of historical data. To found a school on the basis of such requirements would be just as difficult as starting a sports club where being near a world record would be a qualification for entry. It is not surprising, therefore, that the reverence which nowadays surrounds his name is not matched by a rush to work along the paths which he has opened.

Like Darwin, Weber suffered for many years from a myster-ious illness which began with a 'nervous breakdown' when he was 33. He was on sick leave from the University of Heidelberg for six years, and at the age of 39 was put into semi-retirement with the title of Honorary Professor. He did not take up regular teaching again until 1918 when he was 54. The illness, however, did not prevent him from working in military hospital administration during the 1914-18 war. Nor did it prevent him from carrying out his massive studies. It is puzzling that while apparently too ill to deliver two or three lectures per week, he was able to write his monumental tomes. Was he malingering to avoid the tedium of repetitive teaching? It seems unlikely in view of what we know about his character. According to the personal reminiscences of Edgar Salin, the Webers used to hold receptions every Sunday which were veritable seminars devoted to high-powered debates. At the beginning Weber usually was reclining on a sofa as a sick man, listening passively. Eventually, however, he would sit up and make a contribution to the discussion which sounded like a well-rounded lecture. Although apparently documents exist, still withheld from the public, which throw some light on this matter, no published materials permit inferences about possible emotional and sexual disturbances. If such could be diagnosed, we might have another example (like Comte's and Spencer's) which fits Freud's idea that creativity stems from repression and sublimation of sexual desire. However that may be, it seems likely that (like Darwin's) Weber's illness was psychosomatic. His death from pneumonia at the age of 56 proved no organic debility because it took place during the worst epidemic of influenza on record, when millions were carried off.

Neither his nor Darwin's case offers any support for the popular notion that genius is next to madness: they might have had what we call 'hang-ups', but these do not reveal themselves in their works, which are written in a sober and very level-headed manner. It is easy to find contrasting examples: some of the writings of Nietzsche and Schopenhauer, for instance, clearly show a powerful mind going off the rails. There is nothing like that in Weber. Even when reading the articles about the issues of the days where he proffers advice from the standpoint of an old-fashioned German nationalist – that is, the values which I cannot share – I am struck by the soundness of his diagnoses and sobriety of his language. No rantings, *argumenta ad hominem*, fulminations nor appeals to emotions can be found in his writings. Whatever complexes or hang-ups he may have had, he was well able to keep them under control in his work.

1.2 The style

There are many reasons why, though commonly cited and quoted, Weber is seldom understood. The most obvious (though not the most important) is that he died before he finished his major works, some parts of which were left as disjointed notes. His volumes on Confucianism, Hinduism and Judaism were to be

5

followed by studies of Islam and Christianity. It seems likely that the final volume would have contained some kind of general summing up. Actually, the last four chapters of *General Economic History* do provide a kind of summary or conclusion; however, this book was not written by Weber but produced from the notes taken by his students. It is likely, therefore, that he would have prepared an improved version for publication had he lived longer.

A more important reason for the widespread misunderstanding of Weber's thought is his heavy and convoluted style. Though a great scholar and thinker, Weber was a thoroughly bad writer. Indeed, of all the great founders of the social sciences, he scores the lowest in the skill of presentation. In comparison with the lucidity and elegance of Adam Smith, John Stuart Mill or de Tocqueville, Weber appears like a blunderbuss. Even within the Germanic cultural tradition – where ponderous and convoluted style was regarded as a testimonial of academic respectability – Weber seems more obscure than many other writers, and much worse than Engels, Freud, Sombart or Kautsky; though not as bad as Georg Simmel. Reading his main works I had the impression that he never revised what he wrote, as even the volumes of *Religionssoziologie*, published while he was alive, contain many repetitions, not a few self-contradictions (though mostly apparent rather than real) and the arrangement lacks order. Later, I found a confirmation of my suspicions in his biography by his wife Marianne, where she says (to quote Reinhard Bendix's translation):

> He was entirely unconcerned with the form in which he presented the wealth of ideas. So many things came to him out of that storehouse of his mind, once the mass [of ideas] was in motion, that many times they could not be readily forced into a lucid sentence structure. And he wants to be done with it quickly and be brief about it on top of that, because ever new problems of reality crowd in upon him. What a limitation of discursive thought that it does not permit the simultaneous expression of several lines of thought which belong together! Therefore, much must be pressed hurriedly into long involved periods and what cannot be accommodated there has to be put into the footnotes. After all, let the reader take as much trouble with these matters as he had done himself.

Bendix goes on to add:

> In addition, Weber indicated reservations of every kind by the ample use of quotation marks, conditional phrases, and other

linguistic symbols of scholarly caution. He also used italics, differently numbered paragraphs, different type faces and other devices to structure his material and distribute his emphases. Therefore no simplification of sentence structure, terminology and paragraphing in an English translation can remedy the defects of exposition from which the original suffers (Reinhard Bendix, *Max Weber: An Intellectual Portrait*).

Even worse sources of confusion can be found: often Weber changes the subject without any indication. For instance, in one of the passages included in the selection *Max Weber on Capitalism, Bureaucracy and Religion*, the main topic is the Chinese imperial administration. Into it is inserted a paragraph which compares it with certain arrangements in the medieval German empire, but which is written in such a way that most readers would think it is still the Chinese administration that he is talking about. Only with some knowledge of German historical terminology can one see that this paragraph must refer to the German empire and is inserted as a comparison. In my translation I have inserted the word German where it was needed. There are many other examples of this kind of thing. However, whereas with many writers obscurity masks the emptiness of thought, with Weber it is always worth it to struggle through the bush to find the gold underneath. Even the parts which are not his best are worth studying carefully. He is convoluted, often unclear and sometimes wrong but never trivial or given to padding. It is for this reason that trying to interpret Weber is such a fascinating pastime. Every great thinker, of course, deserves attentive study – and it is always interesting to find out more about his character, life, environment and sources of inspiration – but a clearer writer's work calls for less exegesis. Although I have edited some of his writings, I have never been tempted to write a book about Herbert Spencer. Not being an historian, I have no desire to write an intellectual biography; and he is such a clear writer that there is little doubt about what he says, while for an evaluation of where he was right or wrong an article seems to suffice. With a writer of this kind, it is unlikely that a commentator will have enough to say to fill an entire book without slipping into unrewarding summarising, which can be better done by selecting extracts. It is quite different with Weber: often what he says appears to be completely wrong on the face of it because of injudicious choice of terms. However, if we try to figure out what he might be getting at, we can see that it is possible to recast his statements in a way which makes them substantially true. Moreover, it is often possible to correct what appears to be one-sidedness by putting the statement in question into a wider context of what he says elsewhere. For instance, people who have only read his *The Protestant Ethic and the Spirit of Capitalism* (when the other works were not available in English) have criticised him for propounding a religious determinism as one-sided as the economic. Nobody who had read his work on the ancient Mediterranean societies can agree with this criticism. Trying to understand Weber is like piecing together a jigsaw puzzle, the pieces of which have to be trimmed in various places to make them fit.

1.3 The different kinds of writings and their salient features

The writings of Max Weber reflect his extraordinary versatility and fall into several distinctive categories.

(1) The first can be described as more or less straightforward history but of the 'structural' (as opposed to the 'evential') kind, to anglicise Fernand Braudel's useful terms. We can put under this heading his earliest works: the first of which is his doctoral dissertation, *A Contribution to the History of the Trading Associations in the Middle Ages*, published in 1889. Although it is still very far from the comparative perspective of his later works, it shows his pioneering and synthesising mind by striding across the conventional divisions of historiography, as it fits neither the pigeon-hole of economic history nor that of legal history, but studies the interaction between the economy and the law. The choice of the topic reveals the interest in the problem of the conditions of the rise of capitalism which remained in the centre of all his studies. The interest in the interaction between economy and law is even more explicit in his 'Habilitationschrift' – a thesis on the basis of which the right to teach independently at a university was rewarded – as can be seen from its title: *Roman Agrarian History and its Significance for Public and Private Law*. It was published in 1891 which was only two years after his previous book, and when he was 27.

(2) The next category consists of fairly conventional sociological and economic studies of the descriptive kind. One of them is about how the stock exchange works and it was published as a little volume in a series called Göttingen Workers' Library. It seems the least interesting of Weber's publications. Much the same can be said about his excursions into the field of industrial sociology and psychology, as conventionally conceived, which were produced when he was active in the Society for Social Policy and one of the three editors of the *Journal of Social Sciences and*

Social Policy (*Archiv für Sozialwissenschaft und Sozialpolitik*). The first of these studies appeared in 1908 under the lengthy title *Methodological Introduction to the Survey of Selection and Adaptation (Vocational Choices and Careers) of Workers in Enclosed Large Scale Industry*. By 'enclosed' (*geschlossene*) he means 'where work is carried on on the premises' as opposed to sub-contracting or putting out. As always, what he says is intelligent: he warns, for example, against attributing to biological heredity what might be better explained by the environmental influences – a common error at that time. There is nothing particularly original in this piece and the programme of research corresponds more or less to what was being done in Britain at that time. The survey in question was carried out under the auspices of the aforementioned Association and Weber summarised the results in the lengthy article on 'Psychophysiology of Industrial Work' which also reviews other similar studies. His ability to write competently on a subject so remote from his main pre-occupations must inspire admiration – and the article may be of interest to an historian of industrial psychology as an indication of the state of this subject in Germany at that time – but we would be succumbing to 'the halo effect' if we attributed enduring value to these pieces.

Another study which falls under the present heading is 'The Problems of Entailed Estates in Prussia in the Light of Agricultural Statistics and Considerations of Social Policy', where statistical data are used to show that the multiplication of these estates is causing a diminution of the German peasant population in the eastern districts of Prussia and an influx of Polish farm hands from the Russian empire. Weber regards these consequences as highly undesirable, and he deplores the sacrifice of the German national interest to the sectional interests of the landed gentry. He also throws interesting sidelights on what he calls agrarian capitalism (which he opposes because he wants to preserve a large and prosperous peasantry) and the Prussian officialdom: in particular about favouritism in promotions to the advantage of the gentry and the snobbish mimicking of the latter by officials of bourgeois origin. It is a competent piece of work, logical in its recommendation from the viewpoint of the author's values, and a useful document for the historian of Prussia: another feather in Weber's cap, but no evidence of genius.

A pre-occupation with the need to preserve the peasantry – and especially the German peasantry in the eastern provinces – also constituted the main theme of the inaugural lecture delivered in 1894. The proposal to bar the immigration of Polish farm labourers from Russian Poland was logical enough from his standpoint but it was a common call among German nationalists of the time. Equally commonplace was Weber's opinion that 'the aim of our social policy is not to make the world happy but to unite the nation (torn apart by modern economic development) for the hard struggles of the future'. Somewhat more original are the remarks about the inability of the bourgeoisie to take over political leadership because of their obsequiousness towards the gentry. Again, well worth reading, but no basis for putting Weber among the great.

(3) When we come to the third kind of writings – the comments on current affairs written during the First World War and its aftermath and an article on Russia written in 1905 we can see an outstanding mind at work whose opinions often appear by hindsight as prophetic. An opinion on desirability of a course of action implies a judgment about the likely consequences of various possible chains of events, which rests upon assumptions about causal relationships. Here a superior insight into how societies function must help. Let us look at one of the simplest examples. In March 1916 Weber sent a memorandum to the leaders of the parties and to the Ministry of Foreign Affairs against an escalation of submarine warfare. His opposition was based not on ethical but purely pragmatic grounds: especially his assessment of the potential power of the United States which was grossly underestimated by Germany's rulers who, suffering from militaristic tunnel vision, could not imagine that a country where soldiers were few, badly armed and not esteemed, could quickly build a large and competent army and wage war energetically. Weber maintained that it was a folly to risk a certain defeat by provoking the United States for the sake of very uncertain prospects of quickly forcing Britain to seek peace. He wrote to his wife from Berlin: 'It seems to me that we are governed by a crowd of madmen.' The valid prognosis of the behaviour of the American government and nation stemmed from the correct diagnosis of their character, and the immunity of his mind to becoming beclouded by wishful thinking.

Another example of the same kind is the memorandum on war aims written at the end of 1915 (also reprinted in *Gesammelte Politische Schriften*) about the war aims, where Weber argues against the clamour for annexations on purely pragmatic grounds that if carried out, they would leave Germany permanently surrounded by a ring of sworn enemies. He advocates a compromise peace and a deal with Britain based on an 'equitable' division of the spheres of influence. He was no doubt right from the standpoint of his values: hindsight leaves little room to doubt that only such a deal offered a chance of a prolongation of

European dominance in the world, and of Germany and Britain remaining dominant world powers. Weber has shown remarkable foresight in realising that neither Britain nor France, nor even both together, could permanently endanger Germany's position as a great power whereas Russia constituted a threat to its independence. He wrote this just after a serious defeat and a long retreat of the Russian army.

Even more impressive are the longer articles which raise interesting points about the relationship between diagnosis, prognosis, prescription, values and theory (whether explicit or implicit). In particular the two long articles on constitutional reform in post-war Germany contain long passages on the inherent tendencies of bureaucracies and parliaments, and relations between them. Long stretches of general discussions can also be found in the two articles about the prospect of constitutional government in Russia: one written after the revolution of 1905, the other after March 1917 during the brief spell of Kerensky's parliamentarism. In both instances Weber correctly predicted the failure of these attempts because of the absence of necessary social conditions. The main difference between what he wrote about Germany and about Russia is that in the former articles he proposes, while in the latter he merely diagnoses and forecasts. The parts of the political articles which have the character of theoretical disquisitions logically belong to his systematic sociology and have been rightly incorporated into the recent editions of *Wirtschaft und Gesellschaft* by Johannes Winckelman.

(4) The pronouncements on philosophy or general methodology of the social sciences constitute the fourth category of Weber's writings. They were published as articles between 1903 and 1919 with the exception of a twenty-page methodological introduction to *Wirtschaft und Gesellschaft*. All these writings are reprinted in *Gesammelte Aufsätze zur Wissenschaftslehre*. Five of them attracted more attention than anything else Weber wrote with the exception of *The Protestant Ethic and the Spirit of Capitalism*: they put forth the postulates which continue to be the subjects of endless discussions: the first goes under the name of '*Wertfreiheit*', value-freedom, objectivity or ethical neutrality; the second affirms the principle of reducibility of sociological concepts to statements about action of individuals, which has been more recently baptised as methodological individualism; the third concerns the nature and uses of ideal types.

(5) The fifth kind can be described as historical case studies of civilisations, with a comparative slant, focused on the interaction between the economy, political institutions, class structure and

11

religion. In the study of the ancient Mediterranean civilisations he does not say much about religion while paying particular attention to military organisation. This work was written as an entry to an encyclopedia of political sciences (*Handwörterbuch der Staatswissenschaften*, 1909) under the unduly narrow title of 'Agrarian Relations in Antiquity'. The three volumes of *Religionssoziologie* cover China, India and ancient Israel, while *General Economic History* covers Europe, naturally with comparative glances. The essay on *The Protestant Ethic and the Spirit of Capitalism* was published in English translation as a separate book, but is included in the first volume of *Religionssoziologie*, the bulk of which is devoted to China. Logically, it goes with *General Economic History*.

Several features distinguish these books from usual historical reconstructions even of the institutional, social and economic kind. In the first place, they do not merely describe various aspects of society or culture, but show at great length how these are interrelated. In this respect Weber's historical reconstructions resemble the studies of primitive societies by anthropologists of the functional school of Malinowski and Radcliffe-Brown. There are no earlier examples of equally functionalist or holistic treatment of historical material. Perhaps the nearest approximation is *La Cité Antique* by Fustel de Coulanges. Perhaps even more holistic (or functionalist in this sense) is de Tocqueville's *Democracy in America*, but it was based on direct observation rather than historical documents. True, the insistence on relating other aspects of social life to the economy was the chief contribution of Marx and Engels which remains of lasting value; and in this sense Weber was their continuator without, however, sharing their one-sidedness.

The second characteristic which distinguishes Weber's reconstructions from normal books by historians is the overriding interest in explaining rather than merely describing. Not that no historian ever wanted to explain; but most historians are (and even more were) interested mainly in describing – in establishing the facts – and many claim to abhor generalising. Under the influence of theorists like Weber and Pareto this attitude has changed to a considerable extent, but in Weber's time historians who looked for explanations (other than imputations of motives to individuals) were very rare.

The third characteristic which these works share only with de Tocqueville's *Democracy in America* among the classics – and which has been emulated by very few later publications – is the constant recourse to comparisons as an aid in analysing the case in hand. This is something very different from Herbert Spencer's comparative sociology (also practised by other writers who did not use this expression) the essence of which was the surveying of a large number of instances, without focusing on any of them, to substantiate or illustrate a general proposition. In contrast, in the works which fall under the present heading Weber uses comparisons most often to back up an assertion about a connection between features of the same society. The general proposition, which serves as a major premise for the imputation of a causal relationship, often remains unstated.

We may call these writings comparative sociology provided we add a qualification which will distinguish them from the more abstract kind concerned mainly with general propositions. Perhaps 'historical comparative sociology' would be appropriate, while the other kind could be called 'abstract' or 'systematic'.

(6) The contents of *Wirtschaft und Gesellschaft* clearly fit the label of systematic comparative sociology, as there references to concrete cases are made at least mainly (and often only) to substantiate a general proposition. They can be divided into two different kinds, clearly distinguished by Weber himself in the introductory note to *Wirtschaft und Gesellschaft*. The first part of that work (our sixth kind) can be fitly described as morphology or comparative morphology. There Weber sets himself the task of defining and classifying social and economic relations and structures. This work appeared in English as a separate book under the misleading title *Theory of Social and Economic Organisation*. It all depends, of course, on what we mean by 'theory', but normally a classification (or even a set of classification which adds up to a general morphology of taxonomy) is regarded as a stepping stone to or a part of a theory rather than as a self-contained theory.

As a morphologist or taxonomist, Weber found two main followers: Leopold von Wiese (author of *System der Allgemeinen Sozologie*, 1924–6) and Talcott Parsons whose most general work is called *The Social System*. The latter's contribution to the advancement of knowledge is negative because he was a muddled thinker and verbose writer who instilled mumbo-jumbo into the minds of thousands of not very bright academics. Being much clearer, von Wiese did no harm and his elaborate morphology is worth reading, but, like Parsons, he did not have a sufficient range of factual knowledge to attempt fruitfully the daunting task of a Linnaeus of sociology. Furthermore, whereas Weber was classifying as a preliminary step to unravelling casual relations, Wiese and Parsons treated this task as the final goal of scientific inquiry. Wiese clearly said so. It is not surprising that nobody has made any discoveries using their classifications.

13

(7) The remainder of *Wirtschaft und Gesellschaft* belongs to the seventh and last genre. It falls under the general heading of comparative sociology of the systematic rather than historical kind – like the morphology from which it is distinguished by focusing on processes, causes and consequences rather than on forms. Moreover, the analysis centres around abstract concepts like feudalism, bureaucracy, the city rather than historical individual like China or the Greek cities as is the case in his work I call historical comparative sociology. Here Weber studies transformations and their causes: how patrimonialism gives way to feudalism or bureaucracy or guild economy to capitalism and so on. He speaks of how and why bureaucratic machines grow, under which conditions law becomes what he calls 'rationalised', which class tends towards which kind of religiosity and so on. This is certainly grand theory but in contrast to Comte, Marx or Spencer, Weber offers neither a universal key nor a cut and dried scheme: he gropes around universal history trying to make empirical generalisations about regularities of accompaniment or sequence. He is not a neat reasoner: he asserts boldly some general proposition about a uniformity or a tendency and then piles up heaps of data to back it up. Owing to the extraordinary range of his factual knowledge, nothing that he says is baseless but the support by evidence is very much on the intuitive level: there is no weighing up of arguments for and against. Nevertheless, Weber's comparative gropings and rule-of-the-thumb inductive generalisations add up to a marvellous achievement and constitute a mine of insights and clues for exploration.

2 Philosophy of the social sciences

2.1 Objectivity and ethical neutrality

The paradigm of '*wertfreiheit*' – which has been translated as value-freedom or ethical neutrality, but which might also be called the paradigm of non-valuation – has often been misunderstood. Some people interpreted it as enjoining upon the sociologist an Olympian indifference to the ills of mankind. Even apart from anything that Weber wrote, his passionate advocacy of various causes shows that this was not what he had in mind. His paradigm of non-valuation can best be regarded as a methodological and semantic rule for classifying propositions, in accordance with which we classify as scientific only non-hortatory and ethically neutral propositions. Naturally, in view of the emotional loading of all the words which describe human relations, strict adherence to this ideal would silence us for ever. But this is no argument against trying to approach it, because the same is true of ideals such as logical consistency or clarity, which are universally upheld, though only intermittently attained. The validity of a methodological precept is not a matter of truth, but of heuristic utility, and by definition a precept cannot be 'value-free'. We must, then, examine the claim of this paradigm on the assumption that knowledge of social phenomena is valuable.

The first argument in its favour is that, when dealing with matters which arouse our emotions, we must discipline our reasoning, so as to avoid wishful or hate-inspired thinking. The adherence to the canon of non-valuation – i.e. careful separation of judgments of value from judgments of fact – is essential for this purpose. Second, the paradigm in question can be recommended on the grounds of semantic expediency. People differ considerably in their valuations, and it is often difficult to infer from the words of praise or denigration what features the objects exhibit other than the capacity to please or displease the speaker. This difficulty might be obviated if all publications carried as a preamble a full exposition of the author's values, but, plainly, the acceptance of the paradigm of non-valuation provides a far more economical solution. The third reason for recommending it is that by excluding numerous controversial issues, it might enable people who disagree about some values, but share the wish to advance the knowledge of social phenomena, to collaborate in the furtherance of this end. Separation of hortatory from factual judgments commends itself as a method of enhancing objectivity in the sense of the freedom of reasoning from the influence of desires other than the desire to know the truth. Only in this sense can objectivity be approached, if not attained, for obviously no reasoning can be independent of the concepts with which it operates, or of the knowledge on the basis of which it proceeds. Arguments for or against the admission of any given proposition into the body of accepted knowledge cannot, of course, be free from judgments of value: they presuppose positive valuation of truth, consistency and of other ideals of scientific thought. They belong, however, not to sociology itself but to its meta-language, to use the expression current among contemporary philosophers.

The distinction between a judgment of fact and a judgment of value has become one of the cornerstones of philosophy ever since Hume wrote his famous statement that 'reason is, and must always remain, the slave of the passions'. (For the sake of readers unacquainted with philosophic usage, I must add that a judgment of fact may well be untrue. A confusion on this point may be avoided by couching the above distinction in terms less akin to colloquial language: namely, existential *versus* normative statements or propositions.) Though beset by the difficulties of application, due above all to the ubiquitous shading-off of concepts into one another, this distinction underlies the ideal of objectivity. In the development of the methodology of the social sciences it was put into the central place by Max Weber. His arguments, however, can be accepted only in so far as they refer to semantic neutrality which is quite a different thing from practical neutrality. Let me make this distinction clear by a few examples.

In the abstract – from the viewpoint of philosophical semantics – what could be more ethically neutral, *wertfrei*, non-hortatory, non-valuative, call it what you will, than the question of how many people fall into which income bracket? Yet the statistics of income distribution can be regarded as highly inflammable material in a system which claims to have abolished inequality of classes. Even in a country where the discrepancy between the official line and reality does not loom so large, data on the distribution of wealth undergo a highly partisan vetting. When the Conservatives were ruling Britain, Labour Party writers produced a spate of studies arguing that the distribution of wealth was much more unequal than was generally believed, while the Conservatives were picking holes in this evidence. After the Labour Party's ascent to power, its intellectuals stopped belabouring this point; thus showing that from a practical standpoint such statistics are not quite neutral.

If somebody says that Oswald did not kill John Kennedy, he is making a statement which is perfectly neutral semantically, as there is nothing in the accepted meaning of any of the words composing this sentence which indicates that the speaker is either pleased or appalled by this act, or that he welcomes or regrets that it was not Oswald who did it. From a semantic standpoint you could have no purer judgment of fact, more neutral ethically. Yet, as everybody knows this was one of the hottest issues of American politics; and such an utterance might still expose the speaker to the wrath of people who hold an opposed opinion on this seemingly simple matter of fact. Though this could not be inferred from the meaning of the words alone, in the actual context of American politics the utterance in question impugns the honesty of the highest dignitaries of the United States, implies that tremendous power rests in the hands of conspiratorial groups, suggests that American democracy is (at least partly) a sham, and consequently brands the utterer as a subversive, with all the practical consequences which such a label might entail.

Or take another example: what could be more neutral than population statistics? And yet a dispute about the census returns nearly led to a civil war in Nigeria early in 1964. The reason was that, as the party alignments followed regional lines, their relative strength depended on the size of population of each region; and so each regional government tried to swell the count of its citizens by all kinds of tricks. At one moment during the dispute the Premier of the Eastern Region offered to accept the census if his region's count was raised by a million. Admittedly this was a rather extreme instance, but there are innumerable less colourful examples to the point.

If the distinction between judgments of fact and judgments of value could be kept clear, mixing them between the covers of a book or during a speech would no more interfere with the communication and cumulation of knowledge than would an insertion of an exclamation about the beauty of the skies in a book on astronomy. In discussions of human affairs, however, only the most extreme forms of judgments of value and judgments of fact appear as entirely distinct. When we are told that somebody's actions or character are admirable or despicable, we cannot infer the nature of his deed or the traits of his personality without knowing the scale of values of the speaker. Exclamations like 'bastard' or 'bugger' have lost their informative content, referring to an illegitimate birth or specific sexual practices, and have come to be used purely as expressions of hostility and disdain. But epithets like 'liar' or 'coward' do have a factually informative content as well as a hortatory and emotive content; the former would not be applied to someone between whose words and deeds (no matter how abhorrent) no discrepancy could be detected, nor would the latter to someone impervious to fear though addicted to cruelty, duplicity or other repellent vices. To take a further example, the same disposition could be called, according to the speaker's attitude and the scale of values, either 'timidity' or 'prudence', but hardly 'foolhardiness'.

To realise how difficult it is to separate the informative from the hortative ingredient of the meaning, it suffices to look at a word like 'fascism'. The word was invented as the proper name for the followers of Benito Mussolini, and later began to be affixed to the movements which proclaimed their sympathy with the Italian fascists or resembled them in their programme or organisation. The communists have extended the meaning of this label to the point of calling 'fascist' anybody who is not on their side; but the compliment was returned when some people began to call them red fascists. The Russian writer Tarsis even defined communism as a particularly perfidious brand of fascism. So the common denominator of the many uses of this word is purely hortatory or emotive, connoting condemnation. Without knowing the speaker's stance, we can infer nothing about the features of a system or movement when we hear it being called 'fascist'. The same is true of the label 'democratic'. Or take another example: the definitions of 'state' normally contain a persuasive ingredient and often little else. One need not go to great lengths to show that a definition of 'state' as an emanation of the general will tends to instil a very different attitude from that induced by the conception of the state as an instrument for the protection of the rich against the poor. Opinions on such seemingly theoretical questions as whether 'state' originated through a conquest or a contract were often dictated by the attitude to the government of the day.

Another fundamental difficulty about neutrality stems from the inescapable circumstance that neither the requirement of factual correctness nor the canon of semantic neutrality tell us anything about what to include and what to leave out when we are describing a situation.

I can draw a map of a city which shows the locations of museums, schools, theatres and other worthy buildings, as well as one which pinpoints only brothels, dope markets, gambling dens and gaols. Both could be equally true and exact; and there is no reason why one of them should be regarded as less true than the other, or less correct than any other map we might care to draw. Or take a less trivial example: from the standpoint of philosophical semantics a statement that so many schools and hospitals have been built in the USSR is just as neutral or non-hortatory as a sentence about how many millions have died there in the forced labour camps. None the less, a willingness to affirm only the first or only the second or both would provide a good clue to a person's attitude towards that state.

Since the sum total of the traits of any empirical phenomenon is infinity, anybody attempting to describe it must decide (consciously or unconsciously) what to note and what to leave unrecorded, and how much attention and space to give to each mentioned item or aspect. Neither the canons of veracity and exactitude nor the distinctions of philosophical semantics, nor even a recourse to unemotional recondite words, can provide a line of escape from the necessity of making such choices. And as every journalist knows, even a picture of a simple event like an accident or a brawl can be altered out of recognition by picking on one assortment of details rather than another; just as a speech can be utterly distorted by stringing together selected though literally correct, quotations.

An awareness of these difficulties ought not to lead us to the defeatist conclusion that every account is equally unreliable and that we can never know anything: for this is surely untrue, and common sense, formed by experiences of everyday life, indicates that some witnesses are less biased than others, not to speak of the differences in their reluctance to tell outright lies. What does follow from the foregoing arguments, however, is that the ideal of objectivity is much more complex and elusive than some pedlars of methodological gimmicks would have us believe; and that it requires much more than an adherence to the technical rules of verification, or recourse to recondite unemotive terminology: namely, a moral commitment to the search for truth – the will to avoid the temptations of wishful and venomous thinking, and the courage to resist threats and blandishments.

Like a judge evaluating witnesses' testimonies, we cannot

assess the value of data without passing a tacit judgment on the character of the source; because, like him or the detective, we normally deal with information which we cannot personally check – and neither membership of a professional association nor the observance of methodological technicalities guarantees even elementary truthfulness, let alone objectivity in the wider sense defined above. Like a judge, we would never get anywhere if we assumed that every account is equally trustworthy, and that objectivity consists in giving equal weight to all statements, because an impartiality between a truthful witness and a liar amounts to a commitment to half-truths and a connivance at deception.

Every group, every power structure, propagates certain beliefs about its nature, as well as about that of its allies and enemies, which do not correspond to the reality. Consequently, anybody who searches for truth about human affairs and then reveals it cannot avoid treading upon some toes, and can hardly fail to be dubbed as an obnoxious heretic or a dangerous subversive. As there are few issues on which no group holds strong preconceptions, it may be quite impossible to remain absolutely neutral, particularly when (as commonly happens) powerful factions follow the principle that 'he who is not with us is against us'. What is more, a commitment to truthfulness usually entails taking sides because of the enormous variations in self-deception and mendacity among groups and individuals. Thus a resolve to tell the truth commits an inquirer to take a stand against those organisations or schools of thought which delude themselves or resort to deception to a greater extent, and on the side of the opponents less prone to these vices. No honest book on physical anthropology could be neutral in relation to the Nazi ideology, with the fiction of the purity of the German race as its cardinal dogma. Likewise, no amount of reluctance to criticise would prevent an honest comparison of the living conditions of manual workers and of top officials from automatically becoming dangerously subversive in a country where the official mythology claims that social inequalities have disappeared while in reality they have not.

Nobody will be treated as neutral if he reveals what others would like to conceal; and this applies not only to high politics but also to all kinds of other situations, such as an industrial consultant's report on the profitability of a business which may lead to promotion for some while depriving others of their livelihood. So we must bear in mind the distinction between semantic and practical neutrality. The first, though by no means so simple as the claimants to a scientific status in the social studies would have us believe, is attainable at least in principle; whereas the second is out of the question in this world of ours where secrecy, deception and delusion play such an important part in determining human actions, and especially who gets what and how.

Despite the elusiveness of its criteria and the impossibility of attaining it fully, objectivity (which includes impartiality as distinct from neutrality) must remain an essential ideal to guide our endeavours. It is not, to repeat, a simple ideal easily followed by applying a few technical rules, but if we reject it entirely we can only become propagandists or parasites, unless we prefer to become warriors or guerrilleros who, rather than reason, prefer to shoot.

As thus interpreted, Weber's postulate of ethical neutrality becomes a demarcation rule for separating scientific from non-scientific propositions, somewhat similar to Popper's demarcation rule according to which only the propositions which can be refuted by obervations ('falsified' as he puts it) must be included in science. The two rules are related because statements of value (to be precise, of intrinsic value, as distinguished from the instrumental) cannot be refuted: they can be condemned but not shown to be untrue. There is no conceivable evidence which could show the falsehood of a statement like 'there is no reason to worry about the future generations since they have done nothing for us'. We can reject it, but not refute it. Although Weber's postulate can be regarded as a corollary of Popper's demarcation rule, this is an insufficient reason for accepting it because it is by no means axiomatic that the latter is valid.

The unnoticed weakness of Popper's position is that its foundations crumble as soon as we apply his rule to the rule itself. As soon as we do this, we see that the rule does not satisfy the conditions of testability: neither Popper nor any of his disciples have considered how it could be refuted (falsified, in their terminology). By its own criterion, the rule is not a scientific proposition. It can neither be deduced from any theorem of logic or mathematics nor presented as a self-evident axiom, impossible to doubt, since Popper claims to have invented it. By its own criterion, the rule belongs to metaphysics – the set of notions which in the opinion of this school is not worth bothering about. It does not help to say that it is a definition to which the criterion of truth or falsehood does not apply, because then the question arises: why should we follow it? Perhaps it is just a fad. It is usually said that the value of a definition depends on its usefulness. Let us accept this, and assume that accumulation of true general propositions (that is scientific discovery) is the purpose for which the demarcation rule can be said to be useful. But how can we know this?

There is a good reason for accepting Popper's demarcation rule: the history of scientific discoveries shows that they were made mostly by people who intuitively, and at least approximately, followed the demarcation rule long before it was formulated, whereas people who put forth ideas about the world which were not open to refutation by evidence from observation have made no contribution to the body of reliable knowledge called science. The general idea, of course, is not new: it has been said many times that untestable ideas cannot furnish a basis for an advancement of science. It is implicit in what Francis Bacon wrote about the need for observation and experimentation. Popper only added an emphasis and a clearer formulation. Nevertheless, this is a contribution worthy of our admiration because in pure philosophy (which deals with the question of how can we know that we know?) it is exceedingly difficult to say anything in the least new, as it is a field where (to use a slightly ridiculous metaphor) the human mind is trying to pull itself up by its own bootstraps.

It might be added on the margin that the same applies to Popper's idea of hypothetico-deductive methods: neither Popper nor anyone else attempted to validate it by applying this procedure to itself. If it is regarded as an empirical generalisation (like a rule of descriptive linguistic) about what a certain set of people do or have been doing without knowing the rule, then it can only be supported by simple induction: a study of history of science aimed at finding out whether all cases of genuine discovery conform to this model. In fact this is not so even in physics, as Popper's successor Imre Lakatos has shown. It is even less the case in biology where the work of classifying was always important (and a classification can be neither true nor false but only more or less useful) and where many generalisations are merely statistical.

The idea of hypothetico-deductive method fares no better if we treat it as a prescription because we face the same question: why should we follow it? Why should we believe Popper that this method offers the only road to scientific discovery? No more than the demarcation rule can it be deduced from any axiom or theorem of mathematics or logic. It is an empirical recipe, and our faith in it must rest upon the belief that by following it we are likely to get better results than we would otherwise. This belief can only be justified by an inductive generalisation from history of science which only partly supports Popper's view: it is true that some of the most spectacular advances in the most exact of the sciences – physics and chemistry – did conform to Popper's model of hypothetico-deductive method, but even in these fields refutation (or 'falsification' in Popper's terminology) was not always a cut and dried affair. If a statement can be only either wholly true or wholly false, then it is clear that a general proposition can be invalidated by one negative instance, while no number of positive instances can prove its truth. This asymmetry becomes less absolute when falsehood and truth are a matter of degree of approximation or uncertainty. Furthermore, no reasoning can proceed without assumptions, and in establishing the truth about the occurrence of a negative instance, and therefore the falsehood of the general proposition, we cannot avoid assuming the truth of all kinds of other general propositions, all of which are open to doubt in principle, while some of which may be doubted for a good reason. Consequently, the refutation ('falsification') may not be so conclusive. In the final resort, Popper's notion of hypothetico-deductive method boils down to the idea (far from unknown to his predecessors) that the process of scientific discovery entails a constant effort to eliminate logical contradictions.

It appears, therefore, that Popper does not quite realise what he is doing: he thinks that he has discovered or proved something where he is commending a model which has been followed only in some instances of scientific discovery, albeit these instances were the most spectacularly conclusive. A more serious reproach, however, is that the support for his anti-inductivist recipe comes from a very impressionistic inductive generalisation from the history of science. This illogicality is reflected in the title of his main work – *The Logic of Scientific Discovery* – in which he maintains that there can be no such thing as logic of scientific discovery but at best only a logic of 'falsification'. This in no way negates the value of the paradigm of hypothetico-deductive method as a recipe for fruitful research, but it shows that this paradigm offers no escape from having to rely on simple induction in the last instance.

In his earlier days Popper maintained that the theory of evolution was not scientific because it could not be tested by a rigorous application of hypothetico-deductive method. His pronouncements on this topic have been misused by various obscurantists interested in discrediting this theory for the benefit of religious fundamentalism or bastardised anti-rationalist marxism. More recently, however, Popper agreed that the theory of evolution merits the label of 'scientific' and he now regards the findings of fossils which fit the theory as satisfying the requirements of hypothetico-deductive method, albeit they involve 'post-diction' rather than prediction. However, not even a much more watered down version of hypothetico-deductive method can be followed in the social sciences. By the criterion of its applicability these sciences do not exist and what Weber and other luminaries have written is worthless. True, this is no argument against Popper because we cannot take it as axiomatic that there are such sciences or that writers like Weber have in fact advanced understanding. Nevertheless, despite the dreadful corruption of these fields of study (which I have discussed at some length in *Social Sciences as Sorcery*), we need not accept the depressing verdict that it is all rubbish and that the works of Weber constitute no greater contribution to knowledge than Hitler's *Mein Kampf*. Of course, we can define 'science' in any way we like – and the meanings of its dictionary equivalents in other languages diverge considerably from the English usage – but we need a word to distinguish careful and systematic study aimed at discovering causal relations and regularities from anecdotal narratives, gratuitous assertions, propaganda or rantings. There is nothing in its etymology to compel us to restrict the connotation of 'science' to the fields where the greatest exactitude is attainable. There is no reason why we cannot speak of inexact sciences because, like most other qualities, rigour and exactitude are a matter of degree, and it is a disservice to the advancement of knowledge to insist that the fields which are not amenable to the most rigorous procedures must not be studied at all, forgetting that even very inexact knowledge is better than complete ignorance or misconception.

We can avoid having to chose between Weber and Popper, and we can accept and use in the social sciences the latter's paradigms of hypothetico-deductive method and demarcation if we interpret them not as rigid yes-or-no rules, but as ideals which may guide us even though we cannot attain them fully. This entails the assumption that refutability is matter of degree; and that, though normally easier, a refutation may be just as insecure or provisional as an affirmation on the basis of a simple induction. I see no reason to doubt that Popper's methodological recipes are good: the most exact and reliable theories have been produced in the empirical sciences where these recipes have been most rigorously followed, even if unconsciously before Popper. In the inexact sciences, however, we can use them most frequently and profitably as criteria of rejection at the lower level of rigour: we can safely reject a proposition which is so vague that there is no way of confronting it with empirical data, but to insist on conclusive refutability by one negative instance would lead us to discard unreliable and approximate explanations in favour of total ignorance. Take, for instance, Freud's theory that dreams constitute a symbolic satisfaction of repressed desires. It is possible to confront it with observations and accumulated reports none of which is very reliable but which together and on the whole suggest that there is something in it. This evidence also suggests that the theory fits only some dreams which constitute an unknown part (likely to be substantial) of all dreams. It is difficult to imagine how a single observation, no matter how well documented, could refute it.

In their broad structure, Freud's theories on the whole come near to Popper's paradigm of hypothetico-deductive method: certain general principles are postulated from which inferences are made which according to their exponents, are confirmed by observations. The trouble is that the inferences as well as the observations, lack exactitude and reliability, and for this reason lend themselves to interpretations which make them circular and therefore irrefutable. Ought we to discard completely even those theories which explain much that otherwise would remain totally inexplicable? The wisest course seems to be to accept them provisionally with reservations and to be on the look-out for evidence which calls for more modifications or qualifications and may warrant a rejection. As they have fewer units of comparison than psychology, which studies individuals, and as they deal with constellations of circumstances which will not recur, historical explanations are even more difficult to substantiate. We can, however, apply Popper's demarcation principle by discarding those which cannot be confronted and weakened by factual data. The same applies to general theories of comparative sociology like Weber's.

Accepting the interpretation of Weber's postulate of '*wertfrei-heit*' as a demarcation rule rather than a commendation of cynicism or apathy, we can inquire into the reasons for recommending it. The only reason that can be given is that its adoption is conducive to the advancement of knowledge. Unfortunately, the history of the study of society provides a very slender basis for generalising about the effectiveness of various approaches and methods. None the less, it does seem that, in so far as there has been an advance of knowledge, it has occurred through an accumulation of factual information and general ideas which satisfy Weber's paradigm to a greater extent than the common run of pronouncement on human affairs, which are mainly of the valuating or hortatory kind.

In the study of society Weber's demarcation rule completes Popper's: the testability of propositions (or falsifiability, in Popper's terminology) depends on their non-valuative or non-hortatory content which alone can be publicly verified (or falsified) since the feelings of the speaker are not open to public inspection. And since only publicly testable statements can be relied upon in the collective endeavour known as scientific research, it follows that Weber's demarcation rule helps us to sort out statements which might be useful from those which cannot be used for this purpose, at least not without a reformulation.

Weber regards '*wertfreiheit*' as a constituent of 'objectivity', but he does not quite make it clear what he means by the latter. 'Objectivity' can be taken as having two distinct meanings: one refers to an attribute of the knowledge – as when we speak of 'objective' knowledge – while the other connotes the attitude of the reasoner. Using it in the latter sense, we can say that it consists of two dispositions:

(1) The will and the ability not to let one's wishes and feelings influence one's reasoning. This entails the readiness to face unpleasant conclusions and a reluctance to jump to desired conclusions. It is easy to see how Weber's demarcation rule can help here.

(2) The willingness to put one's opinions to test by confronting them with empirical evidence and submitting them to an examination for logical inconsistency.

These dispositions make no sense without the assumption that 'objective' knowledge is attainable: we must assume that it is possible to find out whether propositions are true or false by confronting them with the 'data' of observation. This presupposes the correspondence interpretation of the meaning of 'truth', without which the terms 'testing' and 'evidence' have no meaning. 'Objectivity' as an attribute of a statement can only mean confirmability by publicly observable events. The belief that objectivity in this sense is possible is, of course, the opposite of cognitive relativism, which is the view that there can be no interpersonally valid criteria for deciding whether a proposition is true or false. Although there is no way of refuting it, relativism can be backed by no arguments because they all fall on a self-contradiction: if nothing can be true, then the statement that it is so cannot be true. Some recent writers have cast Weber into the role of a prophet of relativism by misinterpreting (as we shall see in the next chapter) his concept of understanding. This is a misconception: Weber did not doubt that objectivity (in both senses of this word distinguished above) was possible.

2.2 What are we to understand by 'understanding'?

The expression 'understanding sociology' – '*verstehende soziol-*

ogie' – was perhaps the least commendable of Weber's innovations. If taken at any of the commonly accepted meanings of the word 'understanding', it is superfluous, presumptuous and misleading because (since everybody agrees that the aim of sociology is to understand how societies work) affixing to it the label 'understanding' is like speaking of 'watery water', 'human women', 'on-going process' or 'popular democracy' (i.e. 'people's people's rule'). A good pragmatic rule for finding out whether a predicate adds any information is to look for its negative and (if it has one) for its opposite. Applying this test we can at once see that the expression '*verstehende soziologie*' makes no better sense in German than it does in English. Its dismissal, however, should not deter us from trying to figure out what Weber was getting at; for, though often careless and sometimes seriously misleading in his choice of words, he was a great thinker who was far above trying to impress the audience with empty verbiage. Furthermore, although the unhappy expression might be construed as evidence that he was attempting to monopolise the label 'understanding', he nowhere claims that only his brand of sociology merits it. On the contrary, it is perfectly clear from his discussion that he is concerned with the fundamental difference between the study of nature and the study of society or culture. In the former field – according to his famous phrase – we 'explain' while in the latter we 'understand'. There is a contradiction between what he says in the text and the implications of the label, which appears completely pleonastic in the light of his own words because if in all the branches of the study of culture and society we are trying to 'understand', then how can sociology, let alone any particular school thereof, be distinguished from the others by 'understanding'?

The greatest difficulty in discussing this problem is the question of what do we understand by 'understanding'? As with trying to define any other fundamental category of thought, it is very difficult here to escape from going round in circles. Take, for example, Wittgenstein's famous dictum (with which I have a great deal of sympathy): 'Whatever can be said, can be said clearly; what cannot be said must be left in silence'. The trouble here is that Wittgenstein does not make clear what he means by 'clearly': he does not succeed in providing an unambiguous criterion by which we could always judge whether a statement is clear or not. Consequently, he breaks his rule by uttering it. Likewise, Weber does not explain what he means by 'understanding'. His characterisation of the difference between the study of nature and the study of culture makes no sense if we accept the meaning which the words 'to explain' and 'to

27

understand' have in the natural sciences where our ability to explain is said to constitute the fundamental measure of the extent of our understanding. To introduce some clarity into this matter, we must realise that Weber had in mind something much more specific than 'understanding' in its general sense. The nature of the latter has provided the philosophers with their chief problems which are 'how do we know that we know' or 'what do we understand when we say that we understand something?' As Weber made no contributions to pure philosophy, I shall try to avoid entering this field too deeply and I shall only say that I subscribe to the view that our ability to explain is the best criterion of our understanding in the sense of the possession of adequate knowledge. However, to express our knowledge (let alone to test its adequacy), we must have words (or some other signs) and be able to understand them in the sense of knowing what they mean. A meaning is said to be a connection between a sign (a pattern of sounds or shapes) and something else: either other signs or something that has happened, is happening or will happen. 'Understanding' of the meaning of a word does not presuppose the possession of adequate knowledge in the sense of the ability to explain and predict the behaviour of the phenomenon to which this word refers. To avoid confusion, I shall speak of 'comprehension' rather than 'understanding' to describe the knowledge of the meaning of a word, which need not be accompanied by the 'understanding' or adequate knowledge of the behaviour of the thing to which this word refers. I may comprehend the word 'tide'; that is know to what it can be applied, without knowing why there are tides, let alone be able to predict when and where they will come and go.

Now, it is true that our comprehension of the words which describe human traits and actions relies on the assumption that other people's minds are sufficiently like ours to permit inferences about their feelings and thoughts on the basis of our own experiences. Up to a point we do that even with inanimate nature when we speak of 'the angry sea' and 'a gentle wind', and the primitive interpretation of nature was mostly along these lines. The development of science, however, was closely connected with the elimination of anthropomorphism, and expressions like the above are now treated as only metaphoric. Aristotle wrote that 'nature abhors a vacuum', but no modern physicist would attribute to gases or liquids the capacity to feel abhorrence. Modern physics consist of equations which subsume, explain and permit to predict various kinds of measurements. But when physicists communicate their formulae they assume the existence of other minds like theirs in whom these formulae will evoke mental representations similar to theirs, although the terms contained in these formulae refer only to observations which can be confirmed by many observers. Many people can certify that I am 183 cm tall, but no one can confirm my feelings.

There is no prospect that we could eliminate from the social sciences words which refer to human feelings and thoughts. All the names for actions contain implications about volitions. Actually, the latter sentence is true by definition because 'action' is commonly defined as voluntary behaviour which is contrasted with reflexes and involuntary activities, which might be conscious, like sneezing, or unconscious, like blinking or the movements of the intestines. We do not need to dwell on behaviour which is particularly laden with emotions, because even if we take something so impersonal as business correspondence we see that it is full of words like 'intend', 'agree', 'expect', 'undertake', 'demand', and such like, which cannot be comprehended except in the light of our own mental experiences. There is no need to emphasise that the same applies to 'trying', 'ambition', 'angry', 'punishment', 'love', 'cheating', 'conquest', and countless other words of this kind. Many of these carry presuppositions not only about the state of mind of the doer but also about the expectations and feelings of the passive objects of actions, as is the case with the words 'to torment', 'to please' and suchlike.

Despite their strenuous attempts to produce a replica of physics, even mathematical economists keep talking about 'expectations', 'profit', 'exchange' – all of which carry implications about thoughts – especially intentions.

I propose to call 'empathic comprehension' the kind of comprehension which relies on the assumption of analogy between our mental experiences and those of other people, and which results in attributing to other people the thoughts and feelings which we would experience in similar conditions. Weber was certainly not the first to notice that our ability to understand other people's behaviour is based on this process. In *The Theory of Moral Sentiments*, Adam Smith says: 'As we have no immediate experience of what other men feel, we can form no idea of the manner in which they are affected, but by conceiving what we ourselves should feel in the like situation.'

There is no way in which the words which describe feeling, thoughts and sensations could be translated into descriptions of physical states. Reading a chemical formula of a substance will give you no idea of its taste, except in so far as you might guess that it might taste like something else which you have tasted and which it resembles chemically. We can no better imagine the

29

dog's world of smells than he can understand mathematics.

As a philosophical digression, I must add that the assumption that there are other minds like ours is a true *a priori* axiom which can be neither refuted nor proven because any attempt to convince anyone of its truth or falsity presupposes the belief in the interlocutor's existence and that he possesses a mind in which we can evoke certain representations by uttering appropriate words. Meaningfulness is the capacity of words and other signs to evoke representations in minds. The so-called verification theory of meaning can be accepted as a body of rules which enables us to distinguish concepts which lead to reliable knowledge from those which do not. It is wrong, however, to equate meaning with conditions of verifiability because you cannot verify a sentence unless you already know its meaning.

We can perceive only the overt behaviour of others, and we can make sense of it only through emphatic comprehension – 'putting ourselves into other people's shoes' – the correctness of which can never be directly verified. Furthermore, by hindsight we often discover that our assumptions about other people's thoughts and feelings were wrong. How do we know that they ever are right? The proof that empathic understanding must be more often correct than wrong is furnished by the existence of society. Any social order would disintegrate totally within seconds if the people enmeshed in it ceased to be able to predict each other's behaviour. In other words, since there can be no society without co-operation, which requires the ability to communicate and to predict other people's behaviour, the existence of society proves that these necessary abilities also exist; and consequently, that empathic comprehension functions with the necessary (though evidently imperfect) efficacy.

It may be worth remarking on the margin that, looking from this angle, we can also solve the much debated question of whether there are any objective criteria of madness or whether it is simply a label for those who deviate from the beliefs of the majority. Those who accept the latter view see no difference between madness, heresy and innovation; between enforced hospitalisation of the insane and incarceration of dissenters and innovators; or between our inability to understand schizophrenics and our inability to understand a foreign language or a branch of mathematics which we have not learned. Now, I do not deny that there are many shading off and mixed cases where it is difficult to draw the line; and it is equally true that a belief or a manner of behaving may be common in one culture but regarded as a symptom of insanity in another. Thus someone who believes in witches riding on broomsticks will be regarded in our society as a lunatic but would be treated as a man of sound judgment in the sixteenth century. None the less, there is a fundamental difference between the two distinctions; foreigners, believers in other religions, heretics and mathematicians understand one another and co-operate – indeed heterodox and persecuted minorities often display a much higher solidarity than does the majority – whereas lunatics can communicate (let alone co-operate) with one another even less than they can with the nurses and psychiatrists. No society consisting of lunatics could survive for a moment. The inability to co-operate (and at the extreme to communicate) with anyone is the objective test of madness which distinguishes it fundamentally from dissent, opposition or crime.

It remains to be added that empathic comprehension is essential not only in co-operation but also in conflict where much effort is often put into figuring out the opponent's goals, assessing his character and knowledge, and forecasting his moves by imagining what one would do in his place.

Being the foundation of all social life and all communication, empathic comprehension cannot be expunged from the social sciences, and Weber was clearly right in stressing that this is a fundamental difference between them and the natural sciences. His shortcoming was that he did not clearly see – or at least did not make it clear in his methodological writings – that sociology (or any other branch of learning aspiring to study mankind or its works scientifically) begins where empathic comprehension no longer suffices. In other words, whereas the practical common-sense understanding of human behaviour relies mainly (or at least largely) on empathic comprehension, the scientific method is needed for going beyond the knowledge thus attainable.

The everyday understanding of people's actions through empathic comprehension mostly relies on goal-and-means schemes. To a question 'why is he doing it?' we normally get (and are satisfied with) a reply indicating his goal or the steps needed to achieve it. If I ask: 'why is he digging up his lawn?', I shall feel that my understanding has advanced when I am told that he wants to grow tomatoes there – my tacit assumptions being that he believes that digging up the lawn is necessary for growing tomatoes there, and that this belief is correct. If I did not make the latter assumption, I would also want to know why he believes this. In cases normally dealt with in books on history the goal-and-the-means schemes are usually much more complicated and much of the effort of the historian is spent on reconstructing the circumstances to piece together evidence which can be arranged as a-goal-and-the-means-scheme. If you ask why did Hitler's army's main thrust into France go through southern Belgium, the answer will have to include the information about the geography of France and Belgium, the composition, tactics, armament and the spirit of the armies involved, the political set-up, and so on. Weber's analysis of historical understanding on the example of the Battle of Marathon is of the same kind. Such knowledge is valuable but it is pre-scientific in the sense of requiring no theoretical formulations about causal relationships which go beyond what was known to the participants. Such formulations are needed when we try to explain cumulative and unintended consequences of actions.

The simplest example of a collective phenomenon which is there, despite being desired by nobody, is the market price. All the buyers would like it to be lower, while all the sellers would like it to be higher. Most movements of prices can be explained without assuming any changes in the dealers' eagerness to buy cheap and sell dear. Nor would empathic comprehension (or 'verstehen') carry us very far in trying to explain inflation, unemployment, overpopulation or changes in fashions and moral values. The same applies to beliefs. If someone tells us that he believes because he wants to believe, we can infer that his belief is shaky. A true believer cannot help believing. To ascertain what he believes we have to resort to empathic comprehension, but this faculty is of no use when we try to explain why he believes what he does or why the number of people who share his beliefs is decreasing or increasing.

Even in dealing with strictly individual characteristics, we can extend our knowledge beyond common sense only when we go beyond the explanations in terms of intentions. When we see somebody walking towards a washbasin, turning on the tap and putting soap on his palms, we do not need a psychologist to tell us that this man is doing this because he wants to wash his hands. But if he washes his hands several hundred times a day, although his work does not require it, we shall not be able to explain his behaviour by using our faculty of empathic comprehension. Only through systematic research can we find common features in the antecedents or traits of character of people suffering from this incapacitating compulsion, and this knowledge may enable us to discover causal relationships which might explain their behaviour. So, even in psychology, science begins where empathic comprehension no longer suffices.

Despite toying with the label 'die verstehende soziologie', Max Weber did not allow it to constrain his studies. Like everybody else he used empathic comprehension to understand texts describing actions and beliefs, but he did not rely on it when he tried to explain how social structures and systems of beliefs persist or change. For this purpose he embarked upon comparative historical studies and used inductive reasoning. As we shall see later, his method was not very rigorous but decidedly inductive. To regard the '*verstehen*' as the distinguishing mark of his approach is to misunderstand completely the nature of his contribution to knowledge.

In his substantive studies, to repeat, Weber was very much an inductivist who built his generalisations on comparative study of history, albeit his formulations were far from rigorous. He certainly never said that sociological inquiry ought to confine itself within the bounds of empathic comprehension. None the less, his failure to make clear the issues connected with the various meanings of '*verstehen*' has recently provided an encouragement to a trend which advocates a retreat from the fundamental principles of scientific method and panders to the obscurantist and parasitic proclivities of sub-standard academics. One of the sources of this trend was perfectly respectable intellectually: namely the book by Peter Winch, *The Idea of Social Science*, where he argued that in interpreting and describing a social set-up it is illegitimate to use concepts other than those which the observed people use themselves. Winch, incidentally, was simply providing another argument to justify the deep-rooted prejudice of Oxford and Cambridge philosophers and historians against any attempt to study society scientifically. He draws the factual support for his argument from the anthropological studies of Evans-Pritchard who repeatedly stresses that there are no English words which adequately translate the magical and religious notions of the Nuer and the Azande. It is true, of course, that the difficulty of translation grows with the cultural and linguistic remoteness, and that no interpretation, description or analysis can be perfectly reliable, accurate or comprehensive. It does not follow, however, that all such works must be totally misleading and worthless. Indeed, if this were the case, then all the examples which Winch draws from anthropological literature would have to be regarded as fictitious and his arguments would lose all their factual backing.

It is particularly anomalous that such arguments should be advanced by linguistic philosophers because linguistics has been much more successful than anthropology or sociology in discovering rules which the speakers obey without knowing them. It is a notorious fact that only very few (if any) among the people who speak their language correctly know its grammar, whereas a linguistician who has discovered and formulated the rules of the given language may not be able to speak in accordance with them. Likewise, when Radcliffe-Brown discovered the general

33

rules which govern (or underlie) the marriage customs of the Australian aborigines, he did not do it by simply writing down what he was told by them, but by drawing inferences from what he saw and heard. His informants knew who ought or ought not to marry whom, but were not able to formulate any general principles or even to conceive of their customs as forming a system. This kind of work, as well as economics and demography, would have to be abandoned if the limitation in question were to be enforced. Nay, an anthropologist who has studied a people who can only count up to five, would not be permitted to tell us how many of them there are.

A professor of philosophy can go on teaching his subject while arguing that sociology is impossible. But what can we make of people who are maintained by the tax-payers as teachers of or researchers in sociology and yet share this view? Under the banner of so-called ethnomethodology many have abandoned all serious analysis and spend their time on recording overheard conversations – preferably trivialities uttered by morons and drunks. It is a sacrilege (for which Weber can in no way be held responsible) that they invoke his name and the word '*verstehen*' to give a veneer of intellectual respectability to their boring scribbles.

The only sensible conclusion to the questions raised by Weber concerning '*verstehen*' is that the raw materials of the social sciences – the meanings of words referring to individual actions, thoughts and feelings – can be comprehended only with the aid of empathy, which has no place in the study of nature; but that science begins only where it goes beyond empathic comprehension (and therefore common sense) and discovers facts, theories and explanations which could not be known without systematic collection and verification of empirical data and inductive inference.

2.3 Social actions and methodological individualism

One of the most absurd misconceptions about Weber's contribution to knowledge is to see it in something called a theory of social action. According to some versions of this view, this 'theory' consists of the 'discovery' that sociology studies social actions . . . as if anyone sane could ever doubt it. Everyone agrees that sociology is supposed to study the social life of mankind; and since life is a chain of actions, there is nothing else that sociology could study. All structures are patterns of recurrent action. This is true even of solid material objects which, as physics teaches us, consist of packets of energy circulating in the void. A material structure is a pattern of recurrent movements of particles. A social structure and its components – such as laws, organisations, customs, kinship and so on – is an arrangement of recurrent patterns of human interaction. Weber did not put it like this, but his remarks about social actions clearly appear to be designed to counter the common tendency to reify sociological concepts.

Weber had no theory of social action in any acceptable sense of the word 'theory'. Apart from some remarks about mutual comprehension being a prerequisite of interaction, he offered a classification of social actions into four categories: the emotional, traditional, goal-rational and value-rational. In itself a classification explains nothing, and amounts to no more than a mere cataloguing, unless it permits a discovery and formulation of true general propositions. The aforementioned classification fails by this criterion, as neither Weber nor anyone else was able to formulate with its aid any general propositions, with explanatory or predictive power. This is not surprising because the classification itself is defective, as it sins against the elementary logical requirements specified already by Aristotle: that is, it has no single principle of division, the classes do not collectively exhaust the field and they are not mutually exclusive.

The distinction between 'goal-rational' and 'value-rational' is useless because Weber does not tell us what is the difference between a goal and a value; and, as generally used in philosophical discourse, these words are treated either as interchangeable or at least as having a very large overlap. We must therefore discard this subdivision and amalgamate the two 'kinds' of rational actions, taking them to be actions based on a correct decision (in the light of available knowledge) of the means for a given goal. The first question which now arises is: can there be actions which are rational as well as traditional or emotional, or are these types mutually exclusive? The second question is: are there social actions which do not fall under any of these headings?

A choice of a correct course towards a goal – that is, a rational decision – involves scrutinising the available knowledge, surveying various possibilities, forecasting their outcomes, evaluating benefits and disadvantages (i.e. costs). As thus conceived, a rational action is a premeditated and planned action. But what about, say, swerving to avoid hitting a child who suddenly runs across the road? It is not a premeditated action, yet it is rational in the sense of serving the purpose which we have at the back of our minds: we do not want to run over children. And what about actions which are carefully calculated but on wrong premises . . .

perhaps insane delusions: for example, a paranoiac who carefully plans elaborate precautions to avoid persecution which nobody has the slightest intention of carrying out? So we have at least three types of action here: planned actions based on rational decisions, planned actions based on irrational decisions and unpremeditated or even automatic actions which do serve our purposes. And we also have automatic actions which produce the opposite effect from that which we desire.

If by 'emotional' action we mean actions accompanied by emotion, then this attribute neither presupposes nor excludes rationality. A prisoner attempting an escape which he has been planning and preparing for months will experience an extremely strong emotion, but his action may be rational or irrational according to the circumstances. The same can be said about all kinds of other actions where big stakes are at issue. So we see that this criterion is independent of that of irrationality. However, German 'affektuel' can also be translated as 'impulsive' which excludes deliberation.

If by 'rational' we mean based on considered decision, then no impulsive action can be rational; but if by 'rational' we mean adapted to our goal then an impulsive action may be either rational or irrational, according to the circumstances. A man who lost his temper and hit or insulted someone, but gained nothing thereby, while having had to endure the ignominy of appearing before a court, may feel that he has acted irrationally; whereas if he shot a lunatic who was about to murder his child, he would feel that his act was very rational despite all the trouble with the police and the coroner which it occasioned.

Making a distinction between 'traditional' and 'rational' action, Weber seems to have in mind the difference between a peasant who goes on tilling the soil in the way his ancestors did, without ever even considering that it might be done in a different way, and a businessman who thinks of many alternatives and weighs their advantages and disadvantages, and ends by introducing a radical innovation. The latter does more calculation and figuring out, but it does not follow that he acts more rationally than the peasant because their environments (especially the knowledge available to each) are so different. Assuming that the most important goal is to survive, sticking to the old and proven ways may be the most rational course in primeval conditions. Traditional methods are usually a product of a long process of trial and error. Experimentation offers a prospect of success only if it is based on accumulated knowledge which enables one to envisage various possibilities and to forecast with some confidence their outcomes. When knowledge is exiguous, while the safety margin is very small on the level of mere subsistence, the most rational course may be to stick to the ways which have been found to be compatible with survival in the past.

The term 'traditional' is inappropriate as a contrast to 'calculated' or 'planned' because many traditional crafts involve a great deal of thinking out and deciding. Furthermore, this term confuses the antiquity of a pattern of behaviour with the question of whether it does or does not involve much ratiocination. Following a new fashion is in no sense more rational than following an ancient custom. The proper word here is 'habitual', but (as we saw earlier on the example of driving) habitual ('unthought out') behaviour may or may not be adapted to the purpose or purposes which the doer has. An habitual reaction of a seasoned driver may be more 'rational' in this sense than the deliberate efforts of a learner.

The conclusion of all this is that, if we want to have a classification of social action which is better than common sense, we must start anew and we will not get much help from Weber. His historical and comparative analyses, fortunately, do not depend on this classification. So, by discarding it and putting some of his statements into a clearer language, we can enhance the value of his insights.

I have made no comments so far about Weber's general concept of social action because little needs to be said about it, as it boils down to an underlining that social action is interaction between individuals which entails communication and therefore mutual comprehension. One can think of certain exceptions to this: when one is coshed from behind in a dark alley and robbed while unconscious, the social action is unilateral and there is neither interaction nor communication. Such situations, however, are marginal, as even in a case of a hold-up there is plenty of communication (or, if you prefer, of symbolic interaction) involving mutual comprehension. So, although what Weber says about the nature of actions is true, it is certainly not new, as all this was made perfectly clear much earlier by David Hume and Adam Smith or even Plato. Much more useful is Weber's stress on the need to define sociological concepts in terms of actions of individuals. This line of thought is pushed to the extreme by the so-called ontological nominalists who maintain that only individuals 'really' exist whereas groups do not. As I have shown in *Social Sciences as Sorcery*, this is an untenable view, which involves dubious assumptions about what is meant by 'existence'. Weber did not deny the existence of groups; and much more in line with his thought is the methodological (as opposed to ontological) individualism which refrains from making ontological judgments (that is, judgments about the nature of 'reality' or 'existence') and confines itself to advocating a methodological rule. The following quotation from its leading exponent conveys the essential points:

> This principle states that social processes and events should be explained by being deduced from (a) principles governing the behaviour of participating individuals and (b) descriptions of their situations. Whereas physical things can exist unperceived, social 'things' like laws, prices, prime ministers and ration-books, are created by personal attitudes. But if social objects are formed by individuals' attitudes, an explanation of their formation must be an individualistic explanation.
> The social scientist and the historian have no 'direct access' to the overall structure and behaviour of a system of interacting individuals (in the sense that a chemist does have 'direct access' to such overall properties of a gas as its volume and pressure and temperature, which he can measure and relate without any knowledge of gas-molecules). But the social scientist and the historian can often arrive at fairly reliable opinions about the dispositions and situations of individuals. These two facts suggest that a theoretical understanding of an abstract social structure should be derived from more empirical beliefs about concrete individuals. (J.N.C Watkins, 'Methodological Individualism', *British Journal of Philosophy and Science*, 1951)

There can be little doubt that methodological individualism is right in its positive recommendations: the only way of guarding against reification of concepts which denote collective phenomena, and their degeneration into empty sounds, is to indicate individual actions which they entail. Words like democracy, capitalism, liberty, socialism, imperialism, or fascism are so useful for propaganda because most people react to them by mindless approval or disapproval instead of thinking about who does, did or will do what, when and how under the circumstances to which these big words vaguely refer. Unfortunately, although the idea of scientific study of society implies by definition a careful scrutiny of the concepts, many people who are supposed to be practising it are just as gullible as the man in the street. Indeed, in many ways they are even worse, as they manufacture vague generalities which obscure and distort their perception of the world. So Weber and the methodological individualists are perfectly right in insisting that whenever we use a sociological concept we must think of the typical actions which it covers. Actually in everyday life everybody does it when they think of the meaning of names of social positions or roles. When you have to explain to a child or a newcomer what is a quality controller, a chairman of the board of directors, or a tax inspector, there is no other way of doing it but to tell him what such people do and how other people react to their actions. Dealing with names for positions or roles, people usually keep quite well in touch with reality; it is when they employ big and more abstract words, like 'class' or 'freedom', that they tend to remain on the level of vague generalities.

Despite having initiated this line of thought, Weber was less one-sided than the exponents of methodological individualism, who treat it as the fundamental principle, because he did not deny the legitimacy of the opposite procedure – which Watkins calls 'holist' – where the traits of an individual are explained by the nature of the group to which he belongs. If you ask why Bill is so touchy, you may be told that he belongs to an ethnic or religious minority which has been demeaned for generations, or that he is the second youngest son in a large family. The very meaning of the words for individual traits – such as kind, clever, cruel, lazy – entails a reference to a mean for the population or to a moral norm whether generally accepted or merely postulated. A reference to the structure of a group and its norms is even clearer in statements like 'Edward is a good husband but a bad manager', where many tacit assumptions are made about the duties, responsibilities and qualifications with which the behaviour of the individual in question is compared. The methodological individualist will say that the structural attributes of a group rest upon the dispositions of the individuals who constitute it – which is true enough – but it is equally true that these dispositions are there because the individuals who have them are members of the given group. It is true that there would be no Hungarian language if no one had ever spoken it; but it is equally true that no one would be speaking it if the set of phonetic patterns known as Hungarian did not exist. To regard either the group or the individual as more fundamental than the other is analogous to giving a simple answer to the chicken-and-egg question. Not even the evolution of the purely anatomical features of mankind can be explained without taking into account the patterns of co-operation and the accumulation of knowledge without which our species could not have survived.

It seems that methodological individualism was conceived by analogy with physicalism, which is the view that ultimately all knowledge can be 'reduced' to the laws of physics and the statements about the movements of physical bodies. 'Reduced' means here 'deduced from'. I gather that chemistry has been 'reduced' to physics in the sense that the laws of chemical composition can now be deduced from the laws of atomic physics. Deducibility permits a replacement of the statements about units of the given level (here the chemical substances and their properties) by the statements about the units which compose them (here atoms) and their relationships. The debate between the vitalists and mechanists in biology hinges on the question of whether all the structures and functions of an organism can be 'reduced' to statements about the entities dealt with by chemistry and physics.

In an aside in *Social Sciences as Sorcery*, I have mentioned the arguments which invalidate physicalism as an ontological doctrine. None the less, physicalism is a more tenable doctrine than methodological individualism because it proposes the reduction of the statements about structures of the higher order to statements about their components whose characteristics do not depend on their inclusion in or exclusion from these structures. Thus, the properties of an atom of oxygen remain the same when it combines with hydrogen to form water or with carbon to form carbon dioxide. We must also note that steps towards a 'reduction' of biology to chemistry and physics (which are being made by all biologists including those who do not believe in physicalism as a philosophical doctrine) involves a replacement of statements about organic processes by statements about units which do not change in consequence of being involved in these processes: that is, the chemical elements and their volumes, velocities and masses. If the mechanists in biology advocated a reduction of statements about organisms to statements about cells, they would get into the same kind of circularity as the methodological individualists because the properties of a cell depend on the nature of the organism of which it forms a part. No cell in a differentiated organism can retain its characteristics after its separation from the rest. A reduction makes sense only when it proceeds to the level where the units are invariant in relation to various structures into which they enter.

The choice between individualism and holism is a false dilemma as neither is acceptable as the fundamental or final reduction. Both procedures are equally valid and indeed necessary. In explaining collective phenomena we must take into account individual dispositions and the other way round. This means that sociology and psychology are inseparable, there can be no clear frontier between them and neither can claim priority over the other. Weber paid no attention to demarcation disputes. When he learned about Freud, he expressed reservations about the correctness of his theories but thought they were potentially of fundamental importance to sociology. The lesson we can retain from Weber is that any term denoting a collective process or structure must be so construed that the question of whether it does or does not apply to a given situation can be resolved by observing actions of individuals. In other words, for every sociological concept we must have observational criteria of its applicability.

To end this section, I must say a few words about how we can reconcile the above-mentioned principle with Durkheim's dictum that 'social facts are things'. Here again, we must try to figure out what he was getting at rather than accept at its face value this dubious pronouncement. Taken literally, Durkheim's dictum either amounts to an empty affirmation that loosely speaking everything is 'a thing' or to a nonsensical assertion that a marriage or a law is a thing like a chair or a house. Taking into account the way in which he conducted his inductive studies (especially of suicide) we can interpret his dictum less literally as a call for objectivity and the application of scientific method to the study of social phenomena, and a reminder about how durable and massive these phenomena are.

Weber's attitude to sociological concepts can also be reconciled with Durkheim's definition of social facts in terms of constraint exercised upon the individual. This definition cuts out certain actions which Weber and most of us would call social because they affect other people – like choosing a friend or setting up a club. None the less, all large-scale social phenomena appear to an individual as compelling and unalterable. The apparent contradiction, however, dissolves when we think about how the constraints operate: they do not come from outer space but result from human actions. Each single individual is constrained collectively by all the others. The cumulative effect of the attitudes of the others puts on every one of us a constraint which is more unalterable and inescapable than a prison wall.

Though not of quite the same stature as Weber, Durkheim was an original and outstanding thinker. Neither of them ever indulged in empty verbiage, but they were tackling great problems without the benefit of clarifications which the philosophy of science has achieved since their times. Consequently, their formulations appear defective and mutually contradictory if taken too literally. But with a bit of chiselling and rabbeting their contributions can be made to fit together very well.

2.4 Ideal types

It might appear that to talk about an ideal type is like talking about wet water because any type, being an abstraction, is ideal and not real in the sense that a given material object is real: there exists this horse and that, but not a horse in general. The difference between an ideal type and a type pure and simple lies not in the abstractness of connotation but in the definiteness of denotation: whereas the types established by biological systematics have referents which fall under them and nowhere else, this is not the case with ideal types. No horse in general ever lived, but there are many horses which satisfy perfectly the specification of 'horsiness'. In contrast, nothing like a perfectly rational organisation or a frictionless pendulum has ever been observed. The idea behind the concept of ideal type is that social phenomena, in virtue of their manifold and fluid nature, can be analysed solely in terms of the extreme forms of their characteristics, which can never be observed in their purity. Weber was neither the first nor the only person to notice this. Pareto repeatedly emphasised that all concepts of physical sciences are idealisations: that no movement without resistance of the medium has ever been observed (but only surmised in the case of the celestial bodies), that nothing perfectly straight has ever been found, that vectorial analysis assumes movements which never take place, and that social sciences must proceed likewise. As far as social sciences are concerned, the most useful idealisations can be found in the most mature of them, which is not surprising: the concepts of economic theory, such as perfect competition or static equilibrium, provide the best examples of ideal types.

Weber speaks of the concept of ideal type in two incompatible senses. In the opening chapter of his essay on *The Protestant Ethic and the Spirit of Capitalism*, he speaks of the ideal type of Protestant ethic. Now, Protestantism (and therefore Protestant ethics) is not a generic concept defined by its abstract attributes and denoting an open set (like, for example, the concept of dictatorship) but a proper name of a particular cultural entity (or a historical individuum, to use Weber's term) located in time and space. In contrast, in the methodological introduction to *Wirtschaft und Gesellschaft* he states that an ideal type is a generic concept, defined by general attributes, and as examples he gives the concepts of rational behaviour and of pure market, where actions are governed solely by the aim of maximising profit. He mentions the stock exchange as the nearest approximation to the ideal type of a pure market. Now, pure market can be defined in generic terms, without reference to time and place, and is methodologically analogous to the concepts of physics like 'ideal gas' or 'frictionless pendulum', whereas 'the ideal type' of Calvinist ethics is something entirely different and without an equivalent in the natural sciences.

No useful concept can be forged by lumping together two incompatible meanings under one blanket term: we must choose between scrapping the term as incurably ambiguous or confining it to one of its meanings, although even then it remains an open question whether this is the best word. There is little to be said for using 'ideal type' in the generic sense because the terms 'pure' and 'perfect' are used in economic theory in the same sense, and have the advantage of having been more successfully employed there than in any other branch of the study of society. True, the word 'perfect' has often tempted the economists to smuggle their judgments of value under the guise of theoretical propositions. However, we cannot forestall all the foibles by juggling with terminology, and any clear thinker ought to be aware that 'perfect' in this sense does not entail 'desirable'.

It is worth remarking on the margin that it is not only the economists who are prone to this slip of logic: some sociologists, for example, define 'perfect social mobility' as a situation where there is no correlation between the social positions of parents and children, and then tacitly assume (without giving reasons) that such a condition would be the most desirable. This is analogous to the error of the economists who presuppose that 'perfect mobility of labour' is the most desirable: in other words, that it is good if people move from job to job solely in response to the differences in prospective income, disregarding the bonds of kinship, friendship, local loyalties and the need for roots. Given that mobility is positively correlated with crime, mental illness and divorce – and that these phenomena put a great burden on the taxpayers – it is unlikely that even by the purely economic criteria the optimal mobility would be anywhere near 'the perfect'. The same is true of 'the pure market', where the behaviour of the participants is governed solely by the desire to buy cheap and sell dear, and where all other motives, such as generosity or traditional ideas of a 'fair' price are inoperative. There are many 'pure' (though few 'perfectly competitive') markets, but it is very unlikely that a society in which all human relations are governed by pure market mechanisms can be conducive to happiness.

Enough has been said to show that it is possible to use pure or perfect types (or 'ideal' in one of Weber's senses) as analytical tools without transgressing the paradigm of non-valuation. It can also be shown that propositions comprising such concepts need not be untestable, as was claimed by some writers who did not distinguish between Weber's and some economists' improper use of these concepts and their intrinsic merits. A proposition attributing a certain characteristic to a pure type need not be gratuitous even if measurement is impracticable so long as we can rank the cases by the degree of approximation to purity. If the type T is defined by the possession of a feature f to a degree of purity or perfection, and is also said to exhibit the feature x, then we can test this assertion by looking at various cases to see whether the degree of approximation to purity or perfection in respect of the feature f goes together with a higher degree of presence of the feature x. For example: perfect competition may be defined by two conditions: (1) that anyone is free to enter the market; and (2) that the decisions of buyers and sellers are made on the assumption that none of them can affect the price. Now, a well-known theorem asserts that under perfect competition the marginal cost of production equals the price. This theorem is not untestable even though neither perfect competition nor absolute equality of the marginal cost and the price can be seen in reality. Some validation can be achieved if we can show that the more fully the two defining characteristics are present, the lesser tends to be the difference between the marginal cost and the price.

An ideal type in this sense is a perfectly good tool of scientific analysis but it was not an innovation of Weber. In its application to social behaviour it emerged gradually in economic theory, and if we insist on attributing paternity to a single individual, it should be either Augustin Cournot or Leon Walras – both much earlier writers. None the less, Weber can be given credit for insisting that such concepts must be relied on in all the social sciences, although the primacy on this score belongs to Pareto who was perhaps a better methodologist, though greatly inferior to Weber as a discoverer of inductive generalisations and explanations. Pure concepts – notably of pure market economy and pure command economy – have been used by Walter Eucken in his typology of economic systems, while a larger assortment of pure systems can be found in Peter Wiles's *Economic Institutions Compared*. However, there is plenty of scope for pure types outside economics.

'Totalitarianism' can best be construed as a pure type if we define it as a system where the government controls the totality of its subjects' lives. This definition is in harmony with the etymology, avoids making assumptions about features which appear to be contingent (such as terror or doctrinairism) and enables us to use an index which is fairly easy to observe: namely, the extent to which the government allows independent organisations to exist. We can see that no real system has been 100 per cent totalitarian, although the USSR around 1950 was very near the mark. Not even Stalin, however, could control the frequency of adultery, masturbation, smoking or drinking or suppress all the little gangs of thieves. The communist rule in Poland has never reached the same degree of totalitarianism. Even at the height thereof, around 1951, if we gave the USSR a mark of 95 per cent on this score, Poland would get something like 80 per cent. Under Gierek, the index of totalitarianism could be estimated at about 60 per cent – perhaps 5 per cent higher than for fascist Italy before the war, although this is debatable because the matters effectively controlled by the rulers were not quite the same in the two cases. Hitler's Germany should perhaps be given a rating of 85 per cent on the eve of the war and 95 per cent at its end.

It is equally useful to think of a liberal state (in the sense of *laissez-faire*) as a pure type of a social system where the government controls nothing, which means that it does not exist except perhaps as an ornament. Such a system was envisaged as the final goal of social evolution by Herbert Spencer who imagined that eventually all social life would be regulated by voluntary agreements and free associations, with no compulsion of any kind. This view was shared by Proudhon and many other anarchist, syndicalist and socialist thinkers, except that they put a greater stress on mutual aid and solidarity. Marx and Engels also entertained this vision when they spoke of the withering away of the state. Almost needless to say, no such condition has ever been seen except within small tribes without rulers whose cohesion rested upon consensus, strengthened by the factor completely overlooked by the utopian visionaries: constant warring against neighbours. The nearest approximation to pure liberalism (or *laissez-faire*) to be found in a large society is the case of the United States (outside the slave states) between 1812 and the Civil War. Even there, however, there was a government, and although it did not even entirely monopolise the function of maintaining peace and enforcing the law (which tasks were to some extent left to the spontaneous action of the citizens), it did regulate certain very important aspects of social life: through the Homestead Act, for example, it prevented the building up of large estates on the Latin American pattern outside the slave states.

We can also construe pure types of legitimate and illegitimate governments. In the first type people would obey the constituted authorities entirely out of their sense of duty, and compulsion would be superfluous and absent. In the second type the feelings of duty would be entirely absent, and obedience would be motivated solely by the fear of punishment or the desire for reward. Although no examples of these types can be found in absolute purity, some cases approach them closely. Britain between 1940 and 1945 was very near to having purely legitimate government. Poland since the beginning of 1982 and Argentina after the Falklands fiasco come even closer to having purely illegitimate governments with mercenaries coercing the rest of the population, including the conscripts.

Many, probably most and perhaps all typologies in the social sciences ought to be construed in terms of pure types, which we may call 'ideal' if we prefer, so long as we stick to one of Weber's meanings of this predicate. As we saw earlier, assertions about attributes of pure types (other than those implied by the definition) can be made just as testable as any in this field. In contrast, it is not easy to see how testability (be it in the loosest sense of any confrontation with evidence) can be achieved with statements referring to 'an ideal type' in the second of Weber's meaning – that is, an idealised description of an historic individuum. Nor is it easy to see what criteria could be invoked to justify a preference for one idealisation of this kind as opposed to another. With proper (i.e. generic) pure types the criterion of goodness is the same as with any scientific term: namely, whether it helps to discover and formulate true general propositions. In a developed theoretical science reports of observations are expected to be correct and exact, while their importance is judged by the light which they throw on the truth of theories. In a descriptive science only the criterion of factual correctness can be applied, and there can be no objective yardstick for comparing the value of descriptions which are deliberately exaggerated and therefore factually incorrect. An 'idealisation' in this sense is analogous to a caricature which shows only a few traits which have been chosen for exaggeration because they distinguish the object from other people. But there are no objective criteria for judging the merits of caricatures: it is all a matter of feeling and intuition. Every description is 'idealised' in the sense that it is selective: as the number of traits of every real thing is infinite, there can be no full description of anything . . . not even of a grain of wheat, let alone something so complex as a culture. Perfect exactitude is also unattainable but this is no justification for deliberate exaggeration. It is more than doubtful whether entomology could be advanced by relying on caricature drawing of insects, and unless we are given good reason to the contrary, we must presume that the same applies to the social sciences.

Weber merely proclaims the virtues of 'the ideal-typical method' without giving reasons. What is even more important there is little evidence of any such method in his substantive studies. At the beginning of *The Protestant Ethic and the Spirit of Capitalism* he says he is going to give us an ideal type thereof –

presumably of a combination of both. In fact, however, he gives an account, backed by copious quotations, of the attitudes which did actually exist among the people of Puritan New England. What he describes is not a concept constructed by himself for heuristic purposes, but an ideal of an enterprising self-made man as seen through the eyes of Benjamin Franklin upon which many New Englanders were trying to model themselves. In addition to norms which everybody is expected to follow, very enduring collectivity has ideals which are held up as worth striving towards but regarded as not fully attainable by ordinary people, while those who attain them are surrounded by admiration. Sometimes such individuals are called heroes or saints, but even where reverence is more measured, every collectivity – be they naval officers, punk-rockers or scientists – has a notion of an ideal specimen of its social type which it regards as worthy of special admiration. Benjamin Franklin's admonitions are clearly meant as counsels of perfection, but he has no doubt that anyone who follows them will be greatly admired by people around him. So in this case 'the ideal-typical method' boils down to giving an account of the ideal widely held among the Americans north of the Potomac around the time of the birth of the United States. It is true that this set of attitudes – which Weber takes as particularly conducive to the development of capitalism – was more widespread and dominant in the non-slave United States than in any other nation, not only at the time of Benjamin Franklin but until the Second World War. So, it could be said in defence of Weber's notion of 'the ideal-typical method' that it boils down to the probably sound advice that in studying the effects of a given attitude it might be useful to pay special attention to the most extreme examples.

Nor does Weber make much use of the concept of 'ideal type' in the generic sense of a pure or perfect type. Most of his crucial concepts – for instance 'patrimonialism' or 'religion' – are undefined, and of those which are, 'feudalism' seems to be the only concept which he explicitly treats as an extreme form of some kind of continuum. What is commonly taken as 'the ideal type of bureaucracy', is, as we shall see later, no more than a list of the chief characteristics of the civil services in western Europe of his time – especially in France and Germany. So, it appears that although he has (as usual) raised interesting questions, no useful methodological lessons can be distilled from what he says about the ideal types. It is not surprising therefore that he himself pays little attention to his own methodological pronouncements when he tries to explain (or even classify) real social phenomena or makes inductive generalisations.

If we want to classify the forms of social life we can derive much benefit from Weber who stands out among the authors of such classifications by virtue of his tremendous knowledge of universal history, as can be seen by comparing his sketches, full of concrete examples, with the works of Leopold von Wiese (the most assiduous of sociological taxonomists) or Talcott Parsons, which are meagre on factual data despite their bulk. Notwithstanding their marvellous sweep, however, few of Weber's classifications and definitions can be accepted as adequate, while many lack precision and logical consistency. This criticism will be substantiated in greater detail on the examples of his concepts of bureaucracy, rationality, and charisma in addition to what has already been said about the types of social action. Here let me make just a few general comments on a couple of other examples, as it would require a bulky tome to comment on every classification which Weber has produced in his notes published in English as a separate volume under the title *Theory of Social and Economic Organisation* – which is misleading because a theory ought to contain more than classifications and definitions.

One of Weber's shortcomings as a taxonomist is the very uneven attention to definitions. For example: the chapters on bureaucracy and patrimonialism are of about equal length and one follows the other. Yet while he devotes several pages to the meaning of 'bureaucracy' he gives no definition of patrimonialism. He tells us that it evolves from patriarchy, and at various points of the discussion he mentions different features of patrimonialism, the most essential of which appears to be the lack of distinction between the ruler's household and the administration of the state. He does not make it clear what is the relationship between the two concepts: he speaks of 'patrimonial bureaucracy' in the ancient Egypt, which is cited in some contexts as an example of patrimonialism and in others as a bureaucracy. Nor does he delimit the other boundaries of the concept of 'patrimonialism'. He uses it interchangeably with patriarchalism when speaking of the small Teutonic or Semitic kingdoms, while in other passages he applies it to the European absolute monarchies of the eighteenth century and the Chinese empire.

What is equally grave, he often omits to make clear whether the type he is discussing is supposed to be 'ideal' or not. 'Bureaucracy' sometimes appears as an ideal type while elsewhere he applies this term to concrete examples of administrative machines without any reservations. Although Weber does not say so, he treats 'patrimonialism' as a type which is not 'ideal' at all but has many exemplifications which fully satisfy the criteria which it entails.

An even graver fault is that many of his classifications fail to satisfy the fundamental rules formulated already by Aristotle: namely, that a classification ought to be based on a single principle of division at each level, that the classes must be mutually exclusive and must jointly exhaust the universe of discourse. The most important of Weber's classifications – that of the types of rule or domination – sins against all three requirements. He does not say what criterion or criteria lead him to single out these types rather than some other. Compare this with Aristotle, who classifies the types of government in the first place in accordance with the clearly unitary criterion of how many citizens share the power – distinguishing government by one, by a few and by many. Within each type Aristotle distinguishes the sound from the corrupt form. We can ask for more precision and may want a definite ratio to demarcate the rule by a few from the rule by many; or we may feel that it would be better to think of degrees along this continuum rather than of discrete classes, but we can be in no doubt about what the principles of classification are. Another good example of a logical classification is Radcliffe-Brown's classification of kinship systems in accordance with the rules of inheritance where he distinguishes the patrilineal, matrineal, bilateral and double descent. No logical basis of this kind can be detected in Weber's afore-mentioned classification where the types are singled out *ad hoc*. Nor do these types jointly exhaust the universe of discourse. We can think of a number of types of domination – say dictatorship, plutocracy, parliamentary democracy or oligarchy – which could be added but which are neither included nor excluded (whether explicitly or implicitly) by Weber. Actually, elsewhere in his great treatise Weber compares the ancient and medieval democracies; and here the distinction is not logical but chronological. But even the chronological criterion is not followed through, as he does not discuss modern democracy, although when talking about capitalism he often compares ancient capitalism with the modern. What he says about these historical formations is of great importance, and his comparison of ancient with medieval democracies constitutes an essential part of his explanation of the differences between the ancient and the modern capitalism. There is certainly no question of these concepts being ideal types.

It remains to be added that his types of domination do not stand in a genetic relationship and cannot be regarded as stages in either unilinear or multi-linear evolution, and have neither a logical nor a chronological basis. It is no taint on them that they stem from intuition, for all new ideas stem from it. Science,

49

however, must proceed from intuition to order and precision, and for this reason Weber's classifications must be treated as a source of suggestions and a challenge rather than satisfactory final products. Despite the defects of his classification of the types of domination, his discussions under the relevant headings clearly rank among the highest achievements of comparative sociology. Their value, however, stems from the inductive generalisations and explanations which they contain: from what he says about the causes, the necessary conditions, antecedents and effects of social changes and continuities. To pay more attention to his classification than to his inductive generalisations and historical explanations (as so many people do) is to misjudge completely Weber's contribution to knowledge.

3   Presiding substantive ideas

3.1   Stress on open-ended causation

Weber's studies of the influence of religion on economic life are
often said to constitute a refutation of the 'materialist' interpretation of history; and it is true that he pays a great deal of
attention to the causal links running in the direction opposite to
that on which Marx and Engels focused. It is clear, however, that
Weber did not think (and I entirely agree with him) that one
needs to write bulky volumes to refute the dogma of the
unilateral causal efficacy of the economic factors, particularly as
neither the founders nor their disciples ever offered any proofs of
its truth but confined themselves to bare assertions. This dogma
rules out questions about the causes of economic changes; and,
by merely working on such questions Weber showed his rejection
of the dogma.

At the end of his life Weber saw how the marxists have
demonstrated the falsity of their dogma by seizing the political
'superstructure' and then using it to smash the old economic
'basis' and to create a new one. Despite his admiration for Marx
and Engels as originators of many illuminating insights and useful
starting points, Weber regarded their disciples' dogmatism as 'a
scholastic mystification', as he puts it in his article on Rudolf
Stammler, where he also says that equally absurd would be a
'spiritualist' interpretation of history which would regard religion
as an invariably ultimate cause of everything else. He emphasises
that there can be no ultimate or final explanations in science, and
that the boundaries between the economic, political and religious
realms are unclear and merely conventional, needed mainly for
cataloguing. This argument alone suffices to refute any monism
claiming to locate ultimate causes in one of the domains thus

labelled, because what grounds can you have for maintaining that all changes in the domain *A* are due to changes in the domain *B* when you do not know how to delimit one from the other. To begin, we would have to have some definitions of what do 'economic' or 'material' mean, which would enable us to draw a clear-cut boundary.

Rejecting all monisms as equally absurd, Weber asserts that, instead of pursuing a chimera of absolutely final explanations, a scientific study must aim at discovering how various specific forms of one kind of phenomena are related to specific forms in other domains. Far from denying this possibility, Weber goes in great detail into how economic circumstances can influence religious beliefs.

It might be added that the so-called material basis consists of ideas as well as of material objects. The latter are useless without the knowledge of how to use them. A machine given to people who have no *idea* what it is for and how to make it work can have no other function than a rock of the same weight. And before any artifact is made somebody must have an idea how to make it and for what purpose. On the other hand, all human activities rely on material objects, as even pure contemplation depends on the correct functioning of the body and a right physical environment. Hegel's idealism as well as Marx's materialisms amount to making fuss about a spurious dichotomy – which is like quarrelling about whether the inside is generally more important than the outside.

The economic interpretation of history (that is, of past politics) does not depend on the philosophical materialism (in the sense of the belief in the non-existence of minds), but it does imply a view about the motivation of social actions: in particular the assumption that the struggle for wealth determines completely all political alignments and conflicts. The mere fact that many people were ready to die for the sake of honour, patriotism or religion proves that this view cannot be correct. A Hindu dying of starvation while refusing to eat a cow shows the power of convictions.

Putting this problem in terms of ideas *versus* interests is incorrect because interests are also ideas – notions about oneself, one's desires and the means of satisfying them. So again it comes down to a view of motivation: of the relative power of selfish or self-regarding desires as opposed to altruism or adherence to moral principles. In reality human behaviour varies enormously and, although some generalisations can be made on the basis of observation, it is plainly silly to lay down *a priori* dogmas about it.

Though nonsensical when applied to the evolution of societies, the triad of Hegel's dialectics – thesis, antithesis and synthesis – fits well enough various turns of intellectual history . . . which is not surprising since this is what Hegel devised it for, and employed the Greek word which means the art of conducting dialogues. If we take the conventional historiography of the early part of the nineteenth century (with its almost complete neglect of the economic conditions, class structures and conflicts) as the thesis, we can treat Marx and Engels's view of history as the inevitably exaggerated (but at the time useful) antithesis, while Weber represents a mature synthesis where the economic facts, the inequality of classes and their conflicts are given due consideration, but without attributing to them any ultimate primacy. To assess his merit correctly, however, we must bear in mind that a number of much earlier writers (for example, de Tocqueville and Le Play or even John Millar in the eighteenth century) saw the matters in a similar light and studied the mutual dependence and reciprocal influence between the economic conditions and other aspects of social life. Max Weber's achievement consists in adding greatly to the stock of inductive generalisations and explanations in this field.

3.2 Non-predetermined evolution instead of predestinarian evolutionism

Evolutionism still reigned supreme in sociology and anthropology when Weber was writing. Among his contemporaries who are now regarded as great only Pareto (at that time known outside Italy only for his work in mathematical economics) opposed to the ideas of progress and evolution his theory of recurrent historical cycles, the essence of which was the circulation of elites. Although he turned into new paths in his later works (especially on suicide), Durkheim's earlier book on *The Division of Labour* is a version (on some points better but on others worse) of Spencer's evolutionism. I shall not dwell on organicism – the reliance on the analogies between an organism and a society – which accompanied evolutionism in the mind of Herbert Spencer and his followers, most of whom also espoused his *laissez-faire* liberalism (which could well be called anarcho-liberalism) despite the greater logical congruence of organicism with collectivism than with individualism and liberalism. Though apparently buried as out of date, Spencer's vision of the universal principles of organisation, which apply to inorganic, organic and super-organic (i.e. social) realms, has lately been revived under the new name of general systems theory. Congruently with his belief in the specificity of the social sciences, Weber had no time for the organic analogies, but (unlike Pareto) he never rejected the ideas of progress and evolution, although he clearly departed from evolutionism. But what was 'evolutionism'?

Most generally, evolutionism can be described as the focus on the universal and uni-directional trends in mankind's past, present and, presumably, the future. We are not, of course, obliged to stick to this meaning, and can use the term 'evolution' in the simpler sense of gradual and general transformation, but this is not how 'the evolutionists' employed it, assuming not only the irreversibility but also the desirability of the universal trends which they claimed to have discovered and which they expected to continue in the future. These assumptions jointly constitute what is called the belief in progress. Max Weber did not share it. His diagnosis of a global trend towards 'rationalisation', as well as his prognosis of a general bureaucratisation, make him an evolutionist of a sort, but he did not applaud these trends, was not an optimist, and did not confuse the inevitable with the desirable.

Herbert Spencer defined evolution as continuous increase in differentiation and integration of structures and functions. In principle these are numerical variables open to measurement, but neither Spencer nor any of his followers made any attempts in this direction, instead of which they produced classifications of stages of evolution of entire societies or special institutions. It is to Weber's credit that he did not condemn evolutionism, despite departing from it radically, because there is nothing wrong with it in principle. As I have pointed out in my introduction to Spencer's writings, the error of most evolutionists (which he shared to a lesser extent) was that they concentrated on the two aspects of social life – family and religion – where a necessary succession of forms is most difficult to discern, and whose origins must remain an object of pure conjecture. In contrast, when we look at the political, economic and military institutions, we can clearly see the universal historical trend from the small and simple to the large and complex, which conforms exactly to Spencer's notion of evolution. Apart, perhaps, from some of the statements about 'rationalisation', Weber said nothing about universal evolutionary trends, but many of his views imply the assumption of evolutionary sequences: that certain forms have to precede others. It is clear that he believed that patrimonialism must precede feudalism and bureaucracy, and not the other way round: whereas neither feudalism nor bureaucracy constitutes a necessary antecedent of the other, although each can develop into the other under certain circumstances. In other words, patrimonialism can develop into either bureaucracy or feudalism; and feudalism could give way to bureaucracy or bureaucracy to feudalism.

We see, then, that Weber affirmed (or more often implied) certain evolutionary sequences and did not deny – in fact guardedly postulated – the existence of a universal trend in the history of human culture. None the less, he was not an evolutionist because he did not view the past as an inevitable (and in a sense programmed) unfolding but as in some sense accidental: he envisaged the possibility that it all might have turned out otherwise than it has. This viewpoint leads him to treat the different civilisations not as phases or stages along the common route but as alternative outcomes of equal finality, so to speak. Whereas Marx and Engels postulated a predetermined sequence – slavery, feudalism, capitalism, socialism – Max Weber knew that slavery as a mainstay of production, far from having been a stage through which all civilisations pass, was in fact an exceptional phenomenon confined to ancient Greece and Rome. He also knew that, as a form of government based on the contract of vassalage which entails obligations on the lord as well as on the vessal, fully developed feudalism appeared only in Europe and Japan. Nor did Weber look at capitalism as something that had to come out of feudalism. Although he did not formulate his standpoint in the way I am trying to do here, many of his statements imply that he regarded capitalism (together with the other distinctive features of the Western civilisation) as something unique which might not have materialised at all. He thinks – rightly, to my mind – that had the Greeks lost the Battle of Marathon there would have been no Western civilisation as we know it. The same could be said about a number of other battles – such as Poitiers in 732, which prevented the Arab conquest of France. After conquering Russia, the Mongols might, perhaps, have conquered the rest of Europe (as they have China) had Subutai not turned back when he heard of the death of the Great Khan.

Assertions about what would or might have happened had something else not happened are known as counter-factual conditionals. Although not truly verifiable, they are implied by every causal explanation. To give a simple example – if you say that the car hit the lamp-post because its steering wheel came off, you are implying that had the steering been checked and mended, this accident would not have occurred. If you say that the defeat of the Stuarts was a precondition of the development of the parliamentary government in England, you imply that it would not have developed had the Stuarts won. It is clear, therefore, that your opinion about what has been possible will be closely connected with your ideas about what needs explaining, the kind of explanations you will search for and the kind of factors you will consider. Weber's feeling that Western civilisation was in some way an accidental deviation from the normal pattern, and that industrial capitalism might not have developed at all, was the source, I think, of the most original feature of his work: the focus on negative instances – the civilisations where it failed to develop.

There was nothing original in Weber's interest in the rise of capitalism: it stems directly from Marx and Engels, and the issue was much debated at the time, especially in Germany. His contemporary, Werner Sombart, produced a massive two-volume survey *Der Moderne Kapitalismus* in 1902, expanded in successive editions to 6 volumes in 1918, and accompanied by separate studies of the impact of the spirit of enterprise, war, luxury and the role of the Jews. Like everybody else, Sombart traced the development of capitalism, whereas Weber was alone in devoting his attention to its non-development. His only work which deals directly with the development is the essay on *The Protestant Ethic and the Spirit of Capitalism*, which appeared as an article in *Archiv für Sozialwissenschaft* in 1904 and as a book in English translation in 1926. Although it attracted most attention and remains the most widely known of all his publications, it appears slight in the amount of work which it embodies in comparison with the astoundingly packed volumes on the ancient Mediterranean, China, India and Israel. When he died he was preparing a study of another failure of capitalism to rise: namely, the civilisation of Islam.

We might ask why Weber went in for such wide-ranging comparisons while neglecting almost entirely nearer comparisons: why did he not compare the various parts of Europe? True, to some extent he does this when comparing Protestantism with Catholicism, and in his systematic, comparative surveys (such as of feudalism or forms of worship) he brings up material from all over the world; but he never attempts to explain why capitalism failed to develop in Spain, Russia, or Poland, or why the lead passed from Italy to the Rhineland and the Low Countries and then to England. I think that the answer is that, once he had made up his mind that religion constitutes the key factor, he had to look for contrasts in this respect. By comparing Poland and Spain with the Netherlands he could have bolstered up his thesis about the influence of religion, but clearly other factors must be invoked to explain why capitalist enterprise did so much better in France than in Spain or Poland, and in northern Italy than in the southern.

In a way Weber's departure from evolutionism entailed going back to the viewpoint of the writers of the eighteenth century when the fact of progress was sufficiently new and geographically confined to prompt people like Hume and Turgot to inquire why it occurs in certain times and places and not in others. In the earlier parts of the nineteenth century Charles Comte and Thomas Henry Buckle also dealt with this question; but by the time when Weber was writing the progress, as well as the European leadership thereof, were so much taken for granted that the interest in explaining them flagged.

The nineteenth-century evolutionists were not so limited as to give no thought to the question of mechanisms which made progress possible. In the first place they inherited from the eighteenth-century thinkers, such as Condorcet, the view that the cumulation of knowledge was the chief motor of progress. Marx's doctrine, which attributes all social and cultural changes to advances in the mode of production, is a restricted version of this idea because the mode of production is the application of technology which is a form of knowledge. But whereas Hume and Turgot gave some answers to the question of social circumstances under which knowledge can advance, the nineteenth-century writers took the advance for granted and felt no need for explaining it. True, under the influence of Darwin, Herbert Spencer added to the previous explanations of progress (by cumulation of knowledge) the idea of the struggle for survival and selection of the fittest. In particular, he saw in war the agency which produced evolution towards more complex forms of organisation, because larger and more highly organised (that is, differentiated and integrated) units tended to be stronger than the smaller and simpler, and therefore were able to displace them. This theory showed the general mechanism which made progress possible and Spencer applied it most successfully to the earlier stages of civilisation, in particular the emergence of larger states from tribes and small chiefdoms. It could not, however, explain why certain collectivities gained the advantage over others. The expansion of industrial civilisation fitted well enough the theory of evolution through struggle and elimination of the weaker entities, but the theory could not account for its rise in the first place. As the rise of scientific and industrial civilisation constituted the most enormous jump in social evolution, it was a very serious shortcoming of the evolutionists that they took it for granted instead of explaining this tremendous 'mutation'. Weber did try to explain it, and we shall look later at how he went about it.

3.3 The weakest point: the concept of rationalisation

The concept of rationality and rationalisation crops up continuously in Weber's writings, plays a central part in his vision of social evolution . . . and yet remains profoundly unclear. He nowhere defines its general meaning and begins by distinguishing its two kinds: 'goal-rationality' (*Zweckrationalität*) and 'value-rationality' (*Wertrationalität*). This he does in the posthumous note (included in the first part of *Wirtschaft und Gesellschaft* as well as in *Theory of Social and Economic Organisation*) where the distinction in question is appended to his sketch of classification of the types of social actions, where, as we saw earlier, he distinguishes the following: affective, tradition, value-rational and goal-rational. The distinction between 'value-rationality' and 'goal-rationality' is, to repeat, very unclear and seems of dubious value. Value-rationality may best be understood as a consistent pursuit of a clearly formulated ideal. 'Goal-rationality' is simply rationality in the sense in which it is used in technology and management science: namely a calculated and appropriate choice of the best means to attain a given objective.

As an ideal which is pursued is a special kind of goal, 'value-rationality' would appear to be a special kind of goal-rationality. Obversely, however, a goal might also be called 'value', so that we have two words for the same thing. Weber gives the acting in accordance with the principle of marginal utility as an example of goal-rationality, although it would more readily fall under 'value-rationality' (if we were to retain this concept) because the essential feature here is the consistent scale of preferences and the calculability of the degree of attainment of different goals.

Although his concepts of goal-rationality and value-rationality have evoked an endless (and in my opinion fruitless) discussion, Weber completely disregards them in his historical analyses and explanations where not a single reference to this distinction can be found, despite frequent employment of the terms 'rational' and 'rationalisation' without qualifications. True, the fact that he finds no use for the distinction in question constitutes no proof that it is useless, but we can safely follow him in disregarding it because it is logically faulty, as just shown.

Because the word 'rationalisation' is often used roughly in the sense given to it by Freud, I must point out in passing that this is almost the opposite of what Weber is getting at. In Freud's scheme, 'rationalisation' means a process of inventing justifications for one's actions in which the agent himself believes but which the analyst knows to be false, having ascertained through psychoanalysis that these actions are either compulsive or serve an entirely different, unconsciously pursued goal. The classic examples are from post-hypnotic suggestion: when someone does what he has been told to do under hypnosis, and to justify these actions he gives seemingly 'rational' reasons. This is not the place to discuss the validity of Freud's theories, and I mention this only to make sure that no reader acquainted with the Freudian usage will confuse it with Weber's.

When he talks about bureaucracy and industry, he uses 'rationalisation' in the sense not far removed from that in which it is employed by business consultants, who mean thereby a process of reorganising a firm (or streamlining its organisation) in such a way that every arrangement is made to serve the general goal – normally assumed to be the maximisation of profit. The latter assumption is not always made clear and people often talk about rationalisation and efficiency as if these were independent rather than relational attributes. Since the introduction of operational research and other applications of mathematics to management – which entailed the translation of the vague ideas of 'rationalisation' and 'efficiency' into the more precise terms of maximisation of definite variables – it became perfectly obvious that it is illegitimate to talk about 'rationality' and 'efficiency' without specifying the goal or goals because what is a rational and efficient arrangement in relation to one goal may be utterly inefficient, irrational or even counter-productive in relation to another. It was not Weber's fault that he lived before operational research and organisational analysis developed, but there is no excuse for employing these concepts without a greater precision today.

To save the concept of rationality from complete vacuity we must conceive of it as the correct choice of the available means in view of a given goal. The means: include the knowledge which is available. It is not irrational to wander around randomly when you are looking for some place but have no map and cannot find anyone to ask. The same applies to our acceptance of beliefs. It is not irrational not to know where Cuzco is; but, if you want to know, it is irrational to have preconceived conclusions on this matter instead of looking up an encyclopedia. In other words, the criteria of rationality of a decision are the same for cognition as for actions upon the environment. The theory of decisions has added many refinements to this scheme. These concern, in the first place, the multiplicity of goals and the relationships between the degree of attaining them. If having more of one thing entails having less of another, rationality of a decision will depend on correct measurement of the utilities and then calculating which course will maximise the sum of the utilities. Further complications stem from the differences in the likelihoods of outcomes. For example: is it better to opt for a bigger gain which is less likely or a smaller gain which is more likely? Here some tricky questions arise, especially when the likelihoods cannot be equated with probabilities derived from observed frequencies. When there are several variables, while the relationship between any two depends on the relationship of each with other variables, the interaction can become so complex that even the most sophisticated mathematical equations cannot provide an adequate model. The mathematical theory of games was devised to deal with interactions between decision-makers where one has to make a decision knowing that the outcome will depend on how the other players will react; but little guidance can be obtained from this theory in practice when the players are many. It cannot be applied at all to situations where the goals are imprecise and neither the degree of their attainment nor the likelihoods thereof can be measured (i.e. the pay-offs and their probabilities are unknown), which is what happens in politics.

Weber could not have known about these methods because they were invented long after his death. It is not necessary, however, to go into these refinements to show the shortcomings of his use of the term 'rationality'.

An analogy with tools makes clear the vacuity of absolute judgments about 'rationality' without reference to the purpose and the circumstances. Is a band-saw or a bulldozer better (or more rational) than a knife or a spade? Certainly not on a desert island, or even in a modern city if your purpose is to sharpen a pencil or plant roses in your back garden. Is an automated shoe factory more 'rational' than a cobbler's workshop? It is certainly better adapted to making large numbers of shoes quickly, cheaply and with little labour in an industrialised country today, but it would have been irrational (nay insane) to try to set up such a factory a hundred years ago; and it might be perfectly rational to revive the cobbler's mode of production if the supply of machinery, electricity and the modern means of transport dries up.

When Weber speaks of 'rationalisation of the view of the world' as a unique achievement of the Western civilisation, he seems to have in mind what is more often called the rise of science and scientific outlook or the progress of rationalism in the sense of the belief that sense perception and reasoning (rather than faith) are the sole source of knowledge. When historians like Lecky (the author of *The Rise of Rationalism in Europe*) write about the rise of rationalism, this is what they mean by it. To avoid getting confused on another score, we must bear in mind that 'rationalism' in this sense is a wider concept than what is meant by 'rationalism' in the history of philosophy where it is contrasted with empiricism; Descartes being regarded as the founder of the former view and Locke of the latter. In this context the question is whether ratiocination or perception is the ultimate source of knowledge. Either option on this score is compatible with being a rationalist in the wider sense. After this warning against confusing the meanings, we can leave the philosophical question of empiricism *versus* rationalism aside, as it has nothing to do with what Weber was getting at.

Perhaps the most fundamental objection to the use of the term 'rationalisation' as an equivalent of 'scientific and technical progress' is that it obscures the difference between a rejection of the appropriate and available means (above all, knowledge) and their unavailability. It is perfectly rational to try to hammer in a nail with a stone if you have no hammer but not if you have one in front of your nose. It was perfectly rational for Columbus to expect to land in India when he sailed west from Spain, but we would regard as a lunatic anyone who entertained such an expectation today. There was nothing irrational about believing in magic when there was no science to show its falsehood. The term 'rationalisation', as used by Weber confuses the accumulation of knowledge with the attitude to it.

It was, of course, common knowledge long before Weber was born that the Occident was the birthplace of science as well as of rationalism in the sense of the belief that observation and logical inference are the only sources of valid knowledge. Nor does Weber say anything specific about the social conditions of the birth and progress of science. None the less, he has made a great (though indirect) contribution towards explaining this epoch-making process by putting forth new ideas about the rise of capitalism, as capitalism and science rose and progressed in close geographical and chronological association. Regardless of what might be thought about the question of whether this association will persist in the future – or even whether it still exists or has existed during the recent decades – it is an indubitable fact that in the past (at least until the governments became deeply involved with science during the First World War) science progressed only where capitalism was developing and vice versa: in every region which was at the time in the forefront of the development of capitalism important contributions to science were being made. As I hope to show in detail in a work which began many years ago as an over-ambitious PhD thesis, this generalisation applies to the civilisations of Asia as well: the periods of efflorescence of Arabic, Indian and Chinese proto-science coincided with the periods of the most significant development of rudimentary capitalism and of the highest status of the merchants. Therefore every step toward explaining the rise of capitalism must throw some light on the birth and development of science. Despite their mutual dependence, however, the two processes are not identical and have separate as well as common roots. As I cannot enter here into a discussion of this great problem, let me just make the obvious point that the pioneers of science were different people from the businessmen – with very different outlook and motives, and often without any close connections with the world of business. The question of why both types came forth in the same regions at the same times demands further probing. To put both processes – as well as the growth and increasing complexity of the administrative machines – under a blanket term 'rationalisation' does not help to unravel the complicated chains of historical causation.

Nobody would deny that our science, technology and the art of organising collective activities of vast multitudes are more developed than what the Eskimos or the Bushmen had, but I see no way of justifying a claim that our culture or social order in its entirety is more rational than theirs. The destruction of the Eskimos' and the Bushmen's societies proves, of course, that the modern nations are stronger, but I see no merit in using the word 'rational' as a synonym for military or economic power. Furthermore, if we were to exclude from consideration the factor of foreign invasion, and judge cultures by the standard of the prospects of long-term survival in isolation, we would have to conclude that the Eskimo culture was clearly better than ours; if left alone, the Eskimos could have gone on with their way of life for thousands, if not millions of years whereas we are rushing headlong into an imminent danger of self-destruction. From the ecological viewpoint, no other civilisation resembled so much as ours does a man sawing off a branch on which he is sitting. One could say in Weber's defence that he wrote before the dangers of an ecological catastrophe and a nuclear holocaust had appeared. None the less, it was the time when the European states were about to get embroiled in a war from which even the victors came out in reality as losers. The wars of Genghiz Khan, Mehmed the Conqueror or Shaka could with much greater justification be regarded as rational because the victors achieved what they aimed at. Leaving the question of morality aside, and judging their performance from a strictly technical viewpoint, we must conclude that Genghiz Khan, Attila and Shaka were much more rational as political planners, strategists and tacticians than the European statesmen and generals at the time of the First World

War because it is difficult to think of any ways in which the methods and decisions of the former could have been improved upon, given the means (including the knowledge) available to them, whereas Haig, Pétain, Lloyd George, Kaiser Wilhelm and Tsar Nicholas, together with nearly all the other monarchs, statesmen and generals of the warring European states, produced a rare display of fireworks of ineptness and stupidity. Of the leading figures of the era around the Second World War, only Stalin can be credited with having acted rationally in the sense of having consistent long-term aims and achieving them by an appropriate (though immoral) choice of the means. Though venerated as the last embodiment of Britain's glory, Churchill was, in fact, a failure who led his country to a defeat disguised as a victory. Britain entered the war to prevent a formation of a dangerous military empire in eastern Europe but its 'victory' helped to create an even more powerful empire in this region and Britain became dependent on American protection. Witnessing the liquidation of the empire which he cherished so much, Churchill drowned his sorrow in whisky and became a mere figurehead during his second premiership. An entire encyclopedia could be filled with examples of political leaders of recent times (whether elected or dictators) pursuing policies which were counter-productive or even suicidal. Indeed, it seems that political decisions are on the whole more haphazard nowadays than they used to be in the past because the increasing complexity of politico-economic reality makes it more difficult to foresee the consequences of various courses of action. Under pressure to propose remedies, but having no means of knowing what their effects will be, the politicians tend to behave more and more like quacks and sorcerers.

Even if we confine ourselves to technology, we have no grounds for asserting that our technology is more rational than that of the Eskimos. Actually a team from an American anthropological museum which was studying the Eskimo material culture has made an interesting experiment, trying to devise ways in which it could be improved upon in the light of modern knowledge but without using imported goods. They have discovered that within the limits imposed by the climate and the available materials they could invent nothing which would be better than what the Eskimos had.

Apart from implying other errors, Weber's generosity with awarding the mark 'rational' to various aspects of the Western civilisation adds up to a gross exaggeration of the duration of its leadership in science and technology. This mistake was inevitable at the time he was writing, when the history of science and technology in Asiatic civilisations was still a virgin soil, but has become inexcusable in the light of the literature available today. Joseph Needham's volumes on the Chinese science and technology – one of the greatest contributions to historical knowledge ever made – abundantly show that the Chinese were much more advanced in these fields than anyone in the West imagined, and that many inventions which were regarded as made in Europe are in fact of Chinese origin. Around AD 1000 China was superior to Europe by every possible criterion of cultural progress. It still remains true that after Copernicus and Galileo European physics reached a level far above anything the Chinese had; but in chemistry this happened only at the end of the eighteenth century when Lavoisier established its scientific basis. European medicine attained a clear superiority only in the nineteenth century. Until the Industrial Revolution the Chinese were not markedly behind in the technology of manufactures: they were inferior in some fields and superior in others. It must be remembered, moreover, that this 'revolution' took place not in Europe as a whole but in England – the only country where factories employing steam engines could be found in substantial numbers before the nineteenth century. By the middle of the nineteenth century the new mode of production had spread to the other countries of north-western Europe but further east, north and south – in Scandinavia, Russia, the Balkans, Spain, Portugal and Southern Italy – the methods and organisation of production were not much different from what they were hundreds of years earlier and by no means clearly superior to what was to be found in China and India.

Navigation and gunnery were the fields in which some European nations attained earliest and clear superiority over the rest of the world. As far as guns are concerned, however, Europe's neighbours quickly learned to use the Italian invention (based on the Chinese invention of gunpowder) and throughout the sixteenth century the Turkish artillery was second to none. In the military art in general the European superiority dates only from the eighteenth century. Until the siege of Vienna in 1683 it was the Turks who were trying to conquer Europe . . . not the other way round. The Spaniards were able to conquer vast territories in America but could make no progress right on their doorstep in North Africa despite a strong motivation provided by the constant depredations which they had to suffer from the corsairs based there.

The foregoing brief survey – to which many other illustrations could be added – points to Weber's fundamental error which was that of lateral as well as retrospective extrapolation. Understandably assuming that science and advanced technology are products of rational thinking, Weber tried to account for their development in Europe by attributing 'rationality' to various other aspects of the European civilisation, and tracing it back to times long before the rise of science, let alone the Industrial Revolution. Without offering separate evidence, he attributed 'rationality' to the religion of the nations which developed science and invented machines; and, since Christianity had Hebrew roots, he saw elements of 'rationality' in Judaism as well. Strangely, in view of his prodigious knowledge of ancient history, Weber says very little about the Greek science and philosophy, although the affiliation of modern science to them can be easily demonstrated, which is not the case with the teachings of the Hebrew prophets.

Although the ancient Greeks failed to develop properly the experimental method – probably because of the contempt for manual skills engendered by slavery – their contribution to the progress of the art of reasoning was the greatest ever made by any nation or epoch. In logical clarity and subtlety, and in the conception of scientific reasoning, the distance between the best of oriental philosophers and the Greeks is much greater than between the latter and the scientists and philosophers of the modern West. Given that the giant step of laying the conceptual foundations of science was made in the environment of polytheism, and that modern science began to advance only after this heritage was absorbed two thousand years later, Weber's search for Hebrew and Christian roots of scientific thought appears as completely misguided.

One of the possible interpretations of the term 'rationalisation' as a description of a cultural trend or transformation, is to take it to mean a widening of the sphere in which people decide rationally (as opposed to acting impulsively or blindly following the habit) in the sense of making clear (at least to themselves) their goals and carefully weighing advantages and disadvantages of various courses of action and the likelihoods of various outcomes. On this score a comparison of our way of life with that of primitive hunters or peasants yields no unequivocal inference. Scientific and technical progress rests upon the division of labour, one aspect of which is differentiation in respect of the amount of skill and knowledge which people acquire and the amount of reasoning which they do. As is well known, the progress of productivity often entails a reduction of skills needed for many jobs. Even if we leave aside the world-wide cretinisation of the masses by the media which was only in its beginning in Weber's lifetime, we can find plenty of evidence to support a thesis that most people in industrial societies have less need or opportunity to make rational decisions than did primitive hunters or peasants. The difference may be of the same order as that between wild and domestic pigs, if on the modern side we focus on people in the most routinised occupations who spend their leisure gaping at the box or deafening themselves with mechanical music.

Nobody has yet devised a method of measuring such differences, although this seems theoretically feasible. On the basis of inevitably impressionistic observations I am convinced that a primitive cultivator or hunter cannot survive without knowing much more and using his brains much more than does a run-of-the-mill modern employee in a routine job. And we must take into account that many people whose work demands extensive knowledge and a good deal of reasoning spend their leisure in an entirely passive and thoughtless manner. So, if we could obtain an index of the amount of rational decision-making per head, it might not show our society as superior to the so-called savages. I would bet on the Eskimos against any modern nation. What is certain is that there is no clear evidence of any general cultural evolutionary trend which can be described as rationalisation in any other sense than the growth of collectively possessed knowledge and the growth of the number of specialists in applying rational thinking in their particular fields – that is the progress of science and technology including the methods of organising.

One of the circumstances which extenuates Weber's cavalier attributions of irrationality to alien beliefs is that he wrote before the great advances in the study of primitive cultures, when the most influential writer in this field was Henri Levy-Bruhl with his theory of pre-logical mentality, based on evidence of travellers' accounts, as Levy-Bruhl himself never saw a primitive society. But when the anthropologists (after Malinowski had set the example) began to learn the languages and spend long periods on intensive observation in the field, they discovered that the so-called savages were neither so wild nor so daft as appeared to hurried travellers. Malinowski's Trobrianders or Evans-Pritchard's Azande appear just as rational as most people in our midst, given the knowledge which was available to them.

In view of the progress in the relevant studies it would be inexcusable today to follow Weber's understandable error of classifying civilisations and religions in terms of a confused concept of rationality. We need not fall into absurd relativism and try to persuade ourselves that the Azande magic is in no way inferior to modern science. We can accept that scientific reasoning constitutes the highest form of rationality. It does not follow, however, that a civilisation which makes the cultivation of science possible, and which depends on its results for its own existence, has been (or is being) scientifically designed and can be called rational in any clear sense of this word. It is common knowledge that even great scientists and philosophers often act counter-productively and entertain completely unwarranted beliefs on matters which affect their emotions. Furthermore, even a society consisting of people who always made rational decisions would not necessarily be rational in its entirety because people have conflicting goals and constantly thwart each other's purposes. Except in the cases when everybody loses or everybody gains, I do not see how we could justify a judgment that one outcome in such a game is more rational than another. We can set up certain ethical criteria and say that one outcome is better (perhaps in the sense of being juster) than another; but goodness or justice are not the same as rationality.

In many contexts – where he talks about an entire civilisation or outlook on life – we can take Weber's 'rationalisation' to mean the progress of science and the multiplication of its applications. Such a translation takes the mystery out of the concept but makes it trivial because many much earlier writers (Condorcet, for example) were well aware of the importance of the progress of science, while Comte saw in it the chief source of the fundamental social and cultural transformations. Weber's title to greatness rests not on a diagnosis of this trend but on his contribution towards explaining the historical causes (or rather conditions) of its unfolding. This contribution is marred by the over-extended use of the insufficiently precise concepts of rationality and rationalisation, but it can be made less vulnerable by a suitable substitution of terms.

In Weber's grading of religions on the scale of 'rationality' there is an implicit assumption (never formulated explicitly as a general principle) that there must be a harmony between science, methods of production and the art of organisation, on one side, and religion, on the other. This assumption flies in the face of the fact that there is no chronological correspondence in the changes in these realms. During the first millennium of its influence, Christianity presided over a regression in scientific knowledge and in the division of labour. The Christian nations began their accelerating progress only during the last quarter of their religion's existence. And since the dogmas changed little after the first three centuries, why should they be regarded as propitious to the process in question rather than as impediments? The latter view is supported by the long history of the opposition to science from the churches. The Reformation was a fundamentalist revival

67

and initially made this conflict even more acute. As John Mackinnon Robertson has shown in his various writings, Protestantism has turned out to be more propitious to science than Catholicism in the long run not in virtue of the contents of its tenets but because it broke the centralised ecclesiastical power and thereby made the control over thought less effective.

If we take contradiction with the findings of science as the criterion of rationality, we must conclude that Christianity is less 'rational' than Buddhism or Islam, not to speak of Confucianism. The comparison with Hinduism is not clear; the activities of Hindu gods override the laws of physics and biology to an even greater extent than do those of the Christian saints, but (perhaps because the Brahmins were never organised into a centralised hierarchy) Hinduism always accepted many strands and interpretations, some of which were very philosophical and unfundamentalist. The view that everything moves in eternal circles, or that there is an infinity of worlds which have neither a beginning nor an end, is more compatible with what we learn from science than is the book of Genesis. Like many other parts of Judaism and Christianity, the latter story has been incorporated into the teachings of Mohammed, but neither the Jews nor the Moslems are required to believe in the divinity of the founder of their religion or his birth from a virgin. Nor do they contradict the rules of arithmetic by saying that God is one and three at the same time. It could well be argued that the cosmologies of Hinduism, Buddism and Taoism could accommodate themselves more easily than did Christianity not only to Copernicus's dethroning of the earth but even to Darwin's theory of the origin of the species.

If we want to rank the religions in accordance with their compatibility with the findings of science, we must place Confucianism far ahead in the first place. Indeed, its rationalistic and this-worldly outlook has led some scholars to deny that it is a religion. None the less, it certainly is a religion in the etymological sense (which is derived from the Latin word 'to bind') because it undoubtedly did constitute a bond which united many millions during two millennia. However, if we include an anthropomorphic concept of deity and the promise of life after death as essential characteristics of a religion, then we have to conclude that Confucianism was not a religion because to the Confucians, the supreme entity is the Heavens – an invisible and impersonal force rather than a personalised god modelled on the image of a terrestrial despot as in the religions born in the Near East.

When asked about what happens after death, Confucius

replied: 'when you don't know enough about the living, how can you know about the dead?' He never claimed, nor was attributed posthumously by his followers, any powers which could be called supernatural or magical. The Confucians expect no miracles, have no saints and revere their founder not as a deity but as a great teacher. Weber's grading of Confucianism as irrational in comparison with Christianity was a retrograde step in relation to the French philosophers of the eighteenth century (among them Voltaire), who regarded China as a model of rationality, contrasting favourably with the superstitious Europe. Fortunately, Weber has supplied many important insights into the nature of the Chinese society whose value is unaffected by this error. In *What is Taoism?* (Chicago University Press, 1977) H.G. Creel writes, 'as far as the political institutions and the economy are concerned, Weber's mistakes are not fundamental. They are most important in his interpretations of beliefs – which is in a way surprising, as in this area he had better secondary sources at his disposal. The explanation is that here Weber went further than anywhere else in stretching the evidence to fit into his preconception of irrationality and to explain the non-development of 'rational' capitalism in China by showing that the Chinese religion, ethos, law and bureaucracy lacked 'rationality'. Now the consensus of contemporary scholars is that among the pre-scientific civilisations the Chinese was peculiarly 'rationalistic' in any of the widely accepted senses of the word. This remains true even if we follow Weber's own explicit definition of rationality, as opposed to his inconsistent usage of this word.'

In one of the essays reprinted in his book *The Great Tritration*, Joseph Needham makes a similar point:

> The more you know about Chinese philosophy, the more you realise its profoundly rationalistic character. The more you know of Chinese technology in the medieval period, the more you realise that, not only in the case of certain things very well known, such as the invention of gunpowder, the invention of paper, printing, and the magnetic compass, but in many other cases, inventions and technological discoveries were made in China which changed the course of Western civilisation, and indeed that of the whole world. I believe that the more you know about Chinese civilisation, the more odd it seems that modern science and technology did not develop there.
>
> The further I penetrate into the detailed history of the achievements of Chinese science and technology before the time when, like all other ethnic cultural rivers, they flowed into the sea of modern science, the more convinced I become that

the cause for the break-through occurring only in Europe was connected with the special political and economic conditions prevailing there at the Renaissance, and can never be explained by intellectual and philosophical tradition. In many ways this was much more congruent with modern science than was the world-outlook of Christendom.

But – the reader may say – the fact remains that science and technology were created by the Christian nations, and how can we explain this if we reject Weber's attribution of superior rationality to the Christian religion? Could it have been a coincidence? My answer in the first place is that one can show a solution to be faulty without knowing a correct answer. Second, the clue may be sought not in the contents of the dogmas but in the separation between the ecclesiastic and the political power – the unique feature of the Western Christendom which had no parallel in other parts of the world. As Otto Hintze (Weber's one-time colleague) has shown in a masterly essay, this separation was a necessary condition of the limitation of royal power by feudal contracts and elective assemblies. Jointly these circumstances made possible the autonomy of the cities, the high status of merchants and craftsmen, and created areas of freedom where industrial enterprise as well as scientific inquiry could strike roots. As can be seen from various passages, Weber knew very well that the separation of the church and the state was a unique feature of Western Christendom but he did not assign a sufficient weight to this factor in his analysis of historical causation. Perhaps he was sidetracked precisely by his misleading notion of rationality.

To realise how inappropriate it is to attribute a superior rationality to the entire mental climate of early modern Europe, it suffices to recall that this was the epoch of an unprecedented intensification of witch-hunting. Far from being due to a mere cultural inertia, the great witch-hunts of the time of Newton (himself a supporter of'this activity) were not only on a much larger scale than anything that went on before, but also displayed a novel feature of picking mainly on women. Of particular relevance to the problem of rationality was the disregard of various common-sense objections to the beliefs about witches which had been voiced earlier, and even officially sanctioned by the church, but were silenced by mass hysteria and terror during the time in question. As Voltaire repeatedly said, nothing so crazy was ever done in China.

It is also interesting that the witch-hunts were most massive in France and Germany, with Britain in the third place, but almost by-passed Spain whose science and industry were decaying. The burning of heretics and converts from Judaism and Islam, suspected of insincerity by the Spanish Inquisitors, appears as a highly rational activity (which has served the purpose of enforcing the orthodoxy and appropriating wealth) in comparison with the torturing and burning of whimsically picked women, which has all the hallmarks of a bout of collective insanity. Elsewhere I have argued that this craze ensued from the impact of syphilis ('Syphilis, Celibacy and Witchcraft', *Encounter*, May 1982).

There is also another very different meaning which Weber attaches to the term 'rational'. When he talks about 'rational' as opposed to 'irrational' capitalism we can infer from what he says about these formations that he has in mind a difference between the form of capitalism which develops the methods and the quantity of production and one which does not. As we shall see later this distinction is of capital importance and crucial to his explanations of the unique achievements of the Western civilisation, but the terms are just as misleading here as in other contexts. If we want a term which covers technical progress together with the growth of the quantity of production and productive equipment, we do not have to invent a neologism because this is what Marx means by 'development of the forces of production'. When capitalism promotes such development Weber calls it 'rational'. As a less misleading term 'productive' or 'industrial' are available. Although he often uses the term 'irrational' to classify the opposite form of capitalism, Weber provides also a better name for it when he speaks of 'booty' or 'political' capitalism (as the opposite of the 'rational'), where money is invested in arrangements for appropriating wealth which already has been produced rather than in production. The Roman tax-farmers are his favourite example. The term 'political' has the advantage of being less emotive but is not very descriptive. I prefer 'parasitic' which I have used when I followed Weber's insight trying to explain the poverty of Latin America.

Productive work and honest trading are more commendable ethically and, no doubt, more conducive to mankind's welfare then conquest and extortion, but it is not a matter of rationality. From the viewpoint of hedonistic and amoral economic calculation it may be more rational to avoid the cost and effort involved in production and seize the wealth produced by others, if you can get away with it. So, in such contexts we should translate 'rational' by 'industrial' or 'productive' and 'irrational' by 'parasitic' or 'predatory'.

At least equally shaky are Weber's pronouncements attributing rationality to certain types of institutions while denying it explicitly or by implication to others. Thus, 'rational' appears as an attribute of bureaucracy but not of feudalism. He does not substantiate judgments of this kind which must remain vacuous unless a purpose is indicated. We must ask, therefore, for which purpose is a bureaucratic organisation more suitable (or 'rational') than feudalism? If we specify such goals as the maximisation of the ruler's power over the subjects, or of the military strength of the state, or keeping the lower classes in subjection, we can easily see that even within such limits no answer can be given unless we also specify the circumstances under which these structures will operate. We can assume that most rulers desired to maintain or extend their control over their subjects, and they chose the means in accordance with their situation. Feudalism was the only feasible (and therefore the most 'rational') arrangement for ruling an illiterate population thinly spread over a large area, where the division of labour, the towns and currency were undeveloped. There are examples of imitative implantation of bureaucratic structures which soon collapsed and gave way to feudalism because the economic and cultural environment was propitious only to the latter. A good example is the early Japan (during the Nara period), whose monarchs set up an administrative system modelled on the Chinese empire. Japan, however, had no great river valleys with room for large-scale irrigation works, and no canals for transportation and centralised distribution of goods levied as taxes in kind. Consequently, the replica of the Chinese bureaucracy disintegrated (in contrast to the Roman empire without any invasion from outside) and gave way to feudalism.

It would be equally fallacious to classify bureaucracy (even in Weber's sense) as a more rational form of organisation for maximising the strength of the state, as in this respect its merits in comparison with feudalism or what Weber calls 'patrimonialism' (that is, primitive despotism unsupported by an elaborate administrative machine) also depend on the circumstances such as the nature of the weapons and tactics and the economic, cultural and geographic environments. In the eighteenth century the semi-feudal kingdom of Poland and Lithuania was effortlessly carved up by the absolutist and bureaucratic Russia, Prussia and Austria; but in the thirteenth century the centralised bureaucratic Byzantine empire was conquered by the crusaders from the feudal monarchies of western Europe. About four centuries later the vast bureaucratic empire of China was conquered by the Manchus whose tribal kingdom could be described as patrimonial in Weber's sense.

When Weber talks about 'rational' authority or bureaucracy, it can be inferred from what he says about these phenomena that 'rational' can be replaced by 'formally and elaborately organised' and 'rationalisation' by 'the growth of elaborate formal organisations' or 'the process of becoming more elaborately and formally organised'. If we want a snappier phrase we have Spencer's expression 'advance of organisation' by which he means exactly this.

We can see thus that what Weber has done was to lump together the key concepts of his great predecessors under a blanket term. He made the confusion even worse by attaching to it a couple of incongruous meanings, as we shall see in a moment. On the score of conceptual clarity on this point his contribution to knowledge is negative, and we shall do better by going back to Comte, Marx and Spencer. If we want a term which would encompass the progress of knowledge, the development of the forces of production and the advance of organisation, Spencer's 'evolution' is much better than Weber's 'rationalisation'. Just as in biology we can say that a mammalian organism is more highly evolved than that of the amoeba – but not that it is more rational – so in sociology or anthropology it makes sense to say that our society is more highly evolved than that of the cave men but not that it is more rational. True, Spencer defined evolution solely in terms of increasing differentiation and integration of the organs and their functions (that is, the growth of complexity) but we can use it in a wider sense, assuming that this process is linked to the accumulation of knowledge and the development of the forces of production. Though close, the interdependence of these three processes is not absolute, as there is a certain amount of loose coupling. The medieval societies had simpler structures than did the Roman empire, but their technology was more advanced. The Greek science was much better than the medieval but in technology it was the other way round. Nevertheless, by and large the three processes are sufficiently linked to justify a concept which covers them all. 'Evolution' might do, but 'rationalisation' will not. No doubt we could define 'rationalisation' to fit the meaning outlined above, but an idiosyncratic definition would only spread confusion in view of all the other meanings and the etymological roots of this word.

In contrast to the lack of definition of rationality in most contexts, in his sociology of law Weber does explain what he means by defining its opposite. On page 395 of the first edition of *Wirtschaft und Gesellschaft* he says (the translation is mine and not word by word which would be incomprehensible):

> legislation and adjudication can be either rational or irrational; they are formally irrational when the decisions are based on methods other than reasoning, such as oracles or their equivalent. They are materially irrational when the decisions are based not on general rules but on ethical, sentimental or political evaluation of cases.

Here at least we can see what he is getting at, but the proper word for the opposite of what he describes is not 'rational' but 'regular'. Furthermore, the concept of 'materially rational' law is pleonastic. If individual cases are decided according to their 'sentimental or political evaluation' rather than with reference to a general rule, then either there is no relevant law or it is disregarded. In other words we have either the absence or a breach of the law. A 'materially irrational' law – that is a law which is not a general rule – is a self-contradictory notion. Weber himself comes near to recognising the pleonastic character of his explication when he adds: 'Every formulated law is (at least relatively) formally rational.' This is a bit like 'every flower is (at least relatively) flowery'. Furthermore, the rule that an oracle must decide is just as general and definite (materially rational in his terminology) as one which says that the court of appeals must decide. True, you might say that it is irrational to believe in oracles, but then you are passing a judgment not on the law but on religious beliefs; because if you assume that God speaks through the oracles then it is perfectly rational to consult them. If you regard the disbelief in this matter as 'rational' you are using this term not in Weber's sense but in the sense in which it was and is used by people who call themselves rationalists, consider reason and sense perception as the sole sources of knowledge, and dismiss all claims of communication with superhuman beings. If we take the enforcement of the laws (as they are) as the goal in relation to which we shall judge the rationality of the procedures then the recourse to oracles in African tribal courts seems much more effective (and therefore rational) than the taking of statements sworn 'by the Almighty God' in Britain in 1982 when the opinion surveys have shown that most people are not afraid of God's punishment.

It may not be meaningless to debate whether the present French or British procedure is more rational in relation to the goals proclaimed by the legislators or the values accepted by the public because these are not very different in the two countries nowadays. But it makes no sense whatsoever to say that the customary laws of the Barotse or the Zulus are irrational whereas the laws in Britain, France or the USA are rational. Actually, a strong case could be made for the view that the laws of the Barotse were more rational in relation to the goal of preserving the values of their culture than is the case in any Western country today. For example, as judged by the criterion of compatibility with the ethical standards accepted by the majority of the population or with the goals and values proclaimed in the parliamentary debates by the legislators who have passed the Act, the present British divorce law is singularly irrational. No irrationality of this degree can be detected in the rules which regulate matrimonial affairs in any of the number of African tribes with whose customs I am acquainted. Actually, only in relation to the goal of maximising the solicitors' income (taken as the sole criterion) can the present British divorce law be regarded as rational.

Once we replace 'rational' by 'regular and predictable', Weber's argument becomes valid in principle though erroneous on a number of points of fact. He is perfectly right in insisting that market economy (or, if you prefer, capitalism) can flourish only where the consequences of legal transactions can be foreseen with near certainty, as without the security of property and unfailing enforcement of contracts neither the profits nor the costs can be foreseen. If legal obligations can be set aside at somebody's whim, business becomes a sheer gamble. Banks cannot function where the recovery of debts depends on a verdict of an oracle or a trial by battle. But societies where the courts resort to such methods of settling disputes are also too primitive in other aspects of culture (such as technology, literacy or the maintenance of internal peace) for an elaborate division of labour and intensive exchange. It would be, therefore, just as gratuitous to attribute the non-development of capitalism among the ancient Teutons to the 'irrationality' of their law, as to say that the reason why a baby cannot drive a car is because it cannot sit up. A comparison relevant to the question of the rise of capitalism is between Europe in the sixteenth, seventeenth and eighteenth centuries and the great civilisations of Asia and antiquity.

Dealing with China, Weber underestimates the regularity with which the laws were administered during the great epochs of the empire. This is perfectly understandable because, lacking other sources of information, he relied on the judgments of nineteenth-century Europeans about the empire rapidly sinking into chaos. True, various laws hampered business enterprise in China and not only arrested but reversed the rise of the merchant class which reached the zenith of its importance around AD 1000. These laws, however, were made (as rationally as any laws anywhere) by the mandarins for this purpose.

As his contemporary Carl Becker has shown (*Islam und Wirtschaft* (1916), reprinted in *Islamstudien*, vol 1, 1924, and the same point is made by Maxime Rodinson in *Islam et le Capitalisme*, Paris, 1966), Weber also underestimates on this score the Islamic law which affords good protection to property and trade. Very broadly speaking it is true that after the great period of the Islamic civilisation which ended in the thirteenth century, and especially since the eighteenth century, the administration of the law was less regular and predictable in the Islamic land than in the countries of western Christendom, but this was due not to the content of the laws but to their disregard stemming from despotism, unlawful exactions by satraps and soldiers, and the venality of the judges and officials, not to speak of the depredations by invaders. Weber knew very well about all this and he was undoubtedly right in seeing in juridical irregularity a crucial impediment to the development of the market economy in the near East. He clearly did not feel, however, that the former set of circumstances sufficed to account for the latter, and resorted to unwarranted grading of the legal systems on the scale of rationality.

If we felt that we must apply this scale to the legal systems, then the only proper way of going about it would be first to discover whether there is a single purpose which most of the laws appear to serve, and then to find out whether they are adapted to this purpose. If this is the case, we can say that the legal system in question is rationalised in the same sense as a business firm is said to be rationalised when all its procedures are adapted to the purpose of maximising the profits. An application of this criterion leads us to a conclusion which is the opposite of Weber's: namely that the most 'rational' legal codes appear to be those promulgated by clever despots. After Ivan the Cruel and Ivan the Terrible – and even more under Peter I – the laws of Russia were very rational in the sense of being well adapted to the single purpose of maximising the Tsar's internal and external power. The laws of the Ottoman empire at its zenith could also be called rational (or rationalised) in this sense. The laws of England were much more rationalised under William the Conqueror than under Queen Victoria or now. Rationalisation of this kind is, in fact, inversely related to the development of the industrial market economy (or capitalism, if you prefer this word) which occurred only in societies where neither a single individual nor a tightly knit oligarchy was strong enough to subjugate entirely the rest of the population and to shape all (or at least most of) the laws to serve his or their single purpose.

When Weber talks about the legal requirements of capitalism

we can often replace his 'rational' and rationality by 'the rule of law' or 'juridical security'; that is, freedom from arbitrary interference by the wielders of powers with the application of the laws. As Montesquieu discovered more than a century earlier, such a condition depends on the division and balance of power. The latter rules out 'rationalisation' (in the sense of subordination to a single purpose) except at rare occasions of universal consent.

As in sociology of law, Max Weber's use of the concept of rationality in relation to the economy is less indefinite than in other contexts. On page 44 of the first edition of *Wirtschaft und Gesellschaft*, he gives the following definition: 'By formal rationality of an economic activity we mean the amount of calculation which is technically possible and in fact applied.' The first objection to this definition is that it is illogically over-burdened: whatever is 'in fact applied' must be technically possible. On the other hand, what is merely possible but is not applied, cannot be both. Therefore, the criterion of technical possibility is superfluous here and therefore confusing. Second, there is no advantage in employing a mystifying term 'formal rationality' when it is a mere substitute for 'recourse to calculation'. 'Formally rational economic activity' should therefore be replaced by 'calculated economic activity' or simply 'economic calculation'. That this substitution is justified we can see from the next page of Weber's treatise where he says: '. . . money is the most perfect means of economic calculation; that is, the most formally rational means of orienting economic activity.' On this rather obvious point, incidentally, he does not go far enough because the qualification 'the most perfect' is superfluous. Money is *the* means of economic calculation. In a barter economy you can count the goods but you cannot calculate the relationships between the exchange ratios of disparate goods because you have no common unit of measurement.

Weber's definition of 'material rationality' is thus translated by Talcott Parsons (*Theory of Social and Economic Organisation*, p. 170):

> The 'substantative rationality' on the other hand, is the degree in which a given group of persons, no matter how it is delimited, is or could be, adequately provided with goods by means of an economically oriented course of social action. This course of action will be interpreted in terms of a given set of ultimate values no matter what they may be.

As often happens, Parsons mistranslates Weber, having got mixed up about which verb refers to which noun. In consequence the only sense which can be distilled from these cumbrous sentences is that 'material rationality' means satisfaction with the results of economic activity. The following translation from page 44 of the first edition of *Wirtschaft und Gesellschaft* shows that, though unclear, Weber was not so trivial. I have tried to save the text from incomprehensibility by putting his subclauses in parentheses. The insertions between the square brackets are my additions:

> In contrast [to formal rationality] by material rationality [of economic activity] we mean the degree to which the mode of provision (through some form of economic activity) of goods for a group (no matter how delimited) is organised with regard to a definite set of values (whatever these might be) by reference to which this mode will, might or could be judged.

As this piece comes from the unfinished notes found in his desk after his death, we should give Weber the benefit of the doubt and assume that he would not have sent this sentence to the printer in its present shape. None the less, even on a generous interpretation what he says does not add up to much and shows him at his worst.

Adapting Bridgman's idea of operationalism and Popper's principle of falsfiability (which I prefer to call refutability) to the terminology of the inexact sciences, we can formulate the following criteria of admissibility of terms:

1   Every term must be defined in a way which clearly indicates the kind of observable data which will enable us to decide whether it can or cannot be applied to any concrete case.

2   Examples of inapplicability as well as applicability must have been observed or at least imagined in sufficient detail to indicate the essential observable characteristics thereof.

The definition in question fails on both counts because we can neither find nor even imagine an example of economic activity (or of any human activity) which is not organised with regard to some values. So, Weber's definition is useless. His 'material rationality' can be replaced by 'single-mindedness'.

Fortunately this does not make Weber's analyses of historical causation invalid, as they can be made much less open to criticism if we put 'economic calculation' wherever he speaks of 'rationality' of economic relations. Weber is perfectly right in saying that such calculation constitutes a rational procedure but he is wrong in assuming that an extension of the field of its applicability necessarily amounts to an increment of rationality, as it may result from a change in the ultimate goals of life. If spouses begin to calculate the cost of their services to each other, this procedure may be rational from the viewpoint of the goal of maximising the income at the disposal of the given individual, but it cannot be regarded as a rational method of enhancing the solidarity of the family or marital love. Seeing a spread of economic calculation within a family, we would be justified in concluding that its members no longer love one another. Now it would follow from Weber's way of using the terms 'rationality' and 'rationalisation' that the less people are motivated by love, generosity or concern for justice, or even disinterested honesty, the more rational does a society become. Many of his statements contradict such a view; and therefore we see once again that there is a serious inconsistency in his terminology.

Many of Weber's statements – especially where he talks about the Protestant ethic tending to 'rationalise' the way of life – can be made much less open to criticism if we replace 'rationalisation' by 'a widening of the sphere of economic calculation.' The causation, however, is indirect: no prophet of Protestantism called upon his faithful to engage in economic calculation; but by preaching hard work and abstemiousness the founders of Protestantism encouraged thrift and therefore accumulation of capital, thus helping the burgeoning market economy to develop, which then led to a widening of the sphere of economic calculation.

Neither his definitions discussed earlier nor his classification of the types of action provide any ground for attributing greater 'rationality' to the goal of accumulating capital through hard work in comparison with other ways of obtaining wealth or with pursuing other goals of life.

As we shall see later, by and large Weber was right in regarding Protestantism (especially Calvinism) as a stimulant of capitalism but he confused himself by seeing the connection in 'the rationalisation' of the way of life brought about by the former, which was supposed to have paved the way for a 'rational' conduct of business. Weber talks about how the Protestant ethic of work has made people more 'rational'. It has been a commonplace in analytic philosophy since Hume that we cannot classify ultimate ends as either rational or irrational. From this viewpoint a businessman who is prepared to forgo leisure and enjoyments of conviviality for the sake of making money is neither more nor less rational than an artist who chooses to live in poverty for the sake of painting as the spirit moves him, or a ne'er-do-well 'butterfly' who cannot stand the boredom of one occupation and flits from one job or domicile to another. And what is rational about going on working like a slave and living parsimoniously when you have enough to relax and enjoy the pleasures of life? It all depends on what you value most. In a recent article I have argued that the key stimulant of parsimony was the panicky fear of pleasure induced by the epidemic of syphilis which struck Europe at the time of the birth of puritanism ('The Syphilitic Shock', *Encounter*, 1980).

It is irrational (in the sense of illogical) to believe in predestination and at the same time to have an activist attitude to life. If your salvation or damnation has been decided before you were born, then what is the point in working furiously? The belief in predestination (in this context called fatalism) has often been cited as the cause of the stagnation or decay of the Islamic lands; so why should its equivalent be responsible for the Calvinists' industriousness, enterprise and thrift? The apathy attributed to the Mohammedans appears as logically more congruent with this belief, and therefore more deserving to be called rational. Nevertheless, it is likely that the Calvinist doctrine of predestination helped the rise of capitalism in another way: namely that by linking poverty with damnation, thus breaking with the millenarian tradition of the church (which goes to its very beginnings) of regarding poverty as virtuous and inculcating the obligation of giving alms to the poor. As Weber rightly says, the view that the poor are also damned by God enabled the rich to go on accumulating capital unperturbed by remorse. Moreover, by curtailing generosity, this doctrine must have facilitated the inculcation of the habits of industriousness and providence into the poor, as anyone who was unable to earn a living and had no capital would be left to die.

Why did Weber describe the spread of a set of arbitrary and logically incompatible beliefs as 'rationalisation'? Why should believing everything you read in a book be more rational than believing everything you are told by a priest? It is perfectly true that in the life of a businessman – particularly one who is single-mindedly devoted to making money – economic calculation plays a larger part than in that of many other human types. None the less, a scheming politician, a general preparing a campaign or a mafioso organising his gang may put at least as much effort into careful planning, weighing the advantages and disadvantages and their likelihoods. Furthermore, a Spanish hidalgo who prefers to stake his life on an adventure against enormous odds rather than demean himself by working with his hands, or a Kwakiutl big man at a feast of Potlach who destroys laboriously accumulated wealth to gain esteem, are choosing correct means which are in perfect congruence with their values – in other words they are acting just as rationally as the businessman, although it is true that they do less counting. Weber's unfortunate choice of the term seems to have been derived through a pseudo-syllogism: first, economic calculation is equated with rationality in general. The second tacit premise is that whatever institution or belief serves to widen the sphere of rationality (that is economic calculation) must itself be rational. This collection of non-sequiturs must be corrected in order to evaluate properly Weber's analyses of historical causation.

We have found several distinct and sometimes incompatible meanings behind Weber's term 'rationality'. We saw that the reason why Weber lumped so many disparate phenomena under one blanket term is that there is some connection between them if we look at them as conditions or aspects of the rise of industrial civilisation. This rise involved the progress of science, technology and the art of organisation which consists of cumulation of products of correct (that is rational) reasoning. In comparison with all other civilisations, the industrial civilisation based on science undoubtedly enlarged the area where rational thinking is practised. The cumulation of the products of rational thought, however, produces unintended and often opposed effects which cannot be described as rational in any definable sense of this term. Furthermore, the products of rational thought are commonly used for opposite purposes and often in a counter-productive manner. A greater scope for rational thinking and the overall rationality of the entire social structure or culture are two distinct phenomena which do not seem to go together. Neither Weber nor anyone else has shown that they do go together, or even given any reason why we might suppose that they do. We must not, therefore, follow Weber in his rash grading of civilisations on the scale of rationality although we can see what he might have been getting at: namely the enlargement of the area in which rational thinking (especially calculation) is done.

Now, technical and economic progress required the channelling of investment into production rather than spoliation. In other words, this progress was fostered by an industrial orientation of the capitalism as opposed to the predatory or exploitative orientation of which the Roman tax-farming is Weber's favourite example. For this reason, it seems, he calls industrial capitalism 'rational' and the predatory kind 'irrational'.

To develop industrial capitalism required an elaborate legal code (in the wide sense of the word) regularly and predictably administered. For this reason, it seems, a legal system which exhibits these features is labelled by Weber as 'rational' and a development in this direction is described as 'rationalisation of the law'.

Nor can industrial capitalism develop very far without a fairly centralised, elaborately organised and regularly functioning public administration. For this reason, Weber applies the term 'rational bureaucracy' to the administrative machines which have these characteristics, while those which do not have them – which are simpler, less centralised and function less regularly – he calls 'irrational'.

The most obvious condition of development of the market economy (and especially of industrial capitalism) is the use of money and the practice of calculating profit and cost. Therefore, Weber equates economic calculation with rationality, disregarding completely the question of multiplicity, hierarchy and incompatibility of values.

Finally, as the progress of industrial capitalism depends on the prevalence of habits of regular and hard work, saving and productive investment, a way of life distinguished by these features is called by Weber 'rational'. For this reason he regards the monasteries as the centres of economic rationality in the Middle Ages. A religion which effectively inculcates such habits is regarded by him as 'rational', while one which does so to a lesser extent, or not at all, is seen as 'irrational'. As we saw, this is what he seems to be getting at when he talks about Puritanism contributing to the 'rationalisation' of the way of life.

We can see thus that Weber's semantic ragbag contains a guiding thread which, though not exactly logical, consists of associations of reasonable ideas. None the less, lumping them all under one blanket term is the opposite of what is needed for advancement of knowledge. To repeat, even Weber's own writings – especially his explanations of historical processes – are less open to criticism if we replace 'rational' and its derivatives by more appropriate words.

4 Systematic comparative sociology

4.1 Law

Weber's sociology of law – which appears as a chapter in the first edition of *Wirtschaft und Gesellschaft* but constitutes a separate volume in English translation – inspires awe by the breadth of the learning on which it rests. As we saw earlier, he began as a legal historian: he wrote a thesis on the beginning of company law in the Middle Ages (chiefly in Italy) and a book on the impact of the private law on the agrarian history of Rome. By the time he came to write his main treatise he had studied not only the legal history of the chief nations of western Europe but also the codes of Russia (in Russian) and of India and China in translations. The subtitle – *The Law and the Economy* – indicates his focus; and, as elsewhere, his guiding thread is the search for an explanation of the rise of the modern form of capitalism in the West: here by examining how this process was affected by the pecularities of the legal systems.

Traditionally the study of law was concerned with what Weber calls 'dogmatics' and exegesis – that is, the determination of the meaning of the statutes, drawing subsidiary rules from them and the discussion of the sources of their validity. The idea behind sociology of law is to look at the laws like a botanist at plants: classifying the legal systems, explaining why they are what they are, and examining their interaction with other aspects of social life. The first difficulty is how to draw the line between the entities which are supposed to be interacting: the economy and the law. The concept of 'the economy' includes the property relations, which are more or less identical with the law of property, and therefore it overlaps with the concept of 'the law'. We must be able to separate the variables before we can study their interaction. To make a rigorous sociology of law possible much analysis and clarification is still needed; so we cannot criticise Weber for not having provided a solution of this fundamental question. Intuitively, however, he seems to sense the trap and talks about certain general features of the legal systems – such as regularity *versus* arbitrariness of the procedures – rather than about provisions of the law which could be regarded as a part of the structure of the economy.

As laws are rules made and applied by people, there is no *a priori* reason why they should not be adapted instantaneously to the changing circumstances. On the other hand, it has been observed that the laws often persist through a kind of inertia. It is very difficult to judge what weight to attach to this variant of cultural inertia in an explanatory analysis. I suspect that Weber might be over-estimating it when he maintains that the availability of the ready-made Roman law was a crucial factor in the development of capitalism in early modern Europe. We can agree with him that the Roman law was more compatible with the needs of business enterprise than were the customary Germanic laws, which is not surprising since Rome had a capitalist economy when these rules were formulated. The availability of the appropriate legal concepts, however, did not prevent the demise of capitalism in the late Roman empire, and the concepts themselves largely fell into oblivion. A thousand years later they were revived and applied when the growth of business enterprise and of the royal administrative machines have made them useful. But which was the cause and which the effect? No doubt putting it like this is too simple: as these were long historical processes, the most likely relationship between them was mutual reinforcement. Nevertheless, the problem of estimating the relative weight of these factors remains. He points out that all the legal concepts which are essential to modern capitalism – the shares, promissory note, bill of exchange, company and so on – are of Germanic origin. Nevertheless, he thinks that the influence of the Roman law was important indirectly by fostering 'rationalisation' of the law. Considering the vagueness of his concept of rationality, it is not surprising that he confines himself to assertions about this 'rationalisation' and offers no proof that it occurred. Nor does he take into account the fact that industrial (in Weber's terminology 'rational') capitalism developed earliest in Britain and the United States – where the legal systems were much less influenced by the Roman law than was the case on the continent of Europe.

Although he did not supply neat answers to such baffling questions, Weber's merit resides in having revealed the immense complexity of the interaction between the law and other social circumstances. In relation to how this subject was treated before him, his achievement fits the role of a synthesis in Hegelian dialectics. As the initial thesis we can consider the old jurisprudence which treated the law (as in the main jurisprudence still does) as something so to speak disembodied or superhuman, and confined itself to discussions about the normative validity of various interpretations, without inquiring into the social effects of the laws or attempting to explain changes therein. Marx and Engels formulated the antithesis, declaring the law to be a mere epiphenomenon – a reflection of the economic interests dominant in a given society. Possibly under their influence, Max Weber already in his first book went beyond the limits of the jurisprudence and legal history on which he was brought up as a student, but he also knew that it was sheer dogma to assert that the economic circumstances determine the laws rather than the other way round. His synthesis consisted of the study of the interaction of the two factors without any monistic preconceptions.

Many of his explanations of various turns in legal history refer to the play of economic interests. Weber, however, improved upon Marx and Engels by discarding the oversimplified dualistic vision of society which has condemned the writing of so many of their followers to sterility. (Actually, in his better moments – when he writes as a historian rather than a preacher – Marx himself takes into account the separate economic interests of the clergy, officialdom, the peasants and the landed nobility as distinct from the capitalists and the workers.) Of special relevance to sociology of law is Weber's interest in the economic interests of the legal profession – not as a mere appendage of the capitalists but as an independent and cohesive group with considerable power and very specific interests. For example, he attributes the non-codification of the English law to the lawyers' pecuniary interest in keeping it incomprehensible to the laymen.

The second notable feature in Weber's sociology of law is his recognition of the importance of the technical element. A new concept or procedure will not come from extraterrestrial sources: somebody must invent it. Without the invention of the concept of limited liability the joint stock company – that cornerstone of modern capitalism – could not have come into existence. But should we view such an invention as an independent factor, or can we assume that the demand would call forth a needed invention? We are treading here on a very difficult ground full of insoluble counter-factual questions: there is no way of knowing about inventions which could have been made and would have been applied had they been made, but in fact have not been made. In science and technology we certainly cannot explain the sequence of inventions simply by the need. Did not the Romans need guns? Do we not need a cure for cancer? It might be argued that because the legal concepts are simpler than those of science or technology, they are less subject to intrinsic concatenation (or immanent dynamics, if you like) and can be brought forth more readily in response to the demand. Weber assumed that the new legal ideas are also difficult to invent, and that the ingenuity (or the lack thereof) of the lawyers must be treated in historical explanation as an independent (or at least partly independent) factor.

Weber's ideas do not add up to a system . . . which is all to the good. When he comes nearest to offering a master key, he is most open to criticism. As in other parts of his writings, the culprit is the word 'rational' with its derivatives, as we have seen already.

As a feat of scholarship – measured by the amount of assimilated recondite information – Weber's sociology of law is the most impressive part of his writings. With little exaggeration one could describe it as almost superhuman: it is astonishing that anyone could know so much about so many legal systems. It is usually regarded as a full-time job to learn about one body of law. Having kept an eye on publications for a book which would supply a second opinion on the matters treated by Weber, I doubt whether anything like his sociology of law exists in the languages which I can read. Most books on comparative law have a much narrower focus even when written by several authors: they usually deal with contemporary laws in Europe and America, or one cultural area like Africa or the lands of Islam. Histories of law are even more specialised. The most notable exception I have come across is a five-volume book in Polish by Karol Koranyi, called *Universal History of Law* which covers an extraordinary range: ancient Near East, Greece and Rome, western and eastern Europe from the Middle Ages to the nineteenth century, and the United States. Weber is much briefer and more selective but he also deals with Chinese, Hindu, Islamic and Israelite law. Weber's range is covered in John H. Wigmore's *A Panorama of the World's Legal Systems* (Washington DC, 1928). This massive volume, however, is purely descriptive: it contains neither comparisons nor theoretical propositions. Many comparisons can be found in another book of an equivalent range: *Vergleichende Rechtslehre*, by Adolf F. Schnitzer (Basel, 1945). There, however, comparisons are made for their own sake rather than (as in Weber) to support theoretical propositions. In keeping with its title, Schnitzer's book is not a sociology of law: it does not deal with the relationships between law and social structure. On the other hand, none of the publications under the heading of sociology of law approaches even remotely Weber's range of factual data. The one which comes nearest to it is also the oldest: Eugen Ehrlich's *Grundlegung der Soziologie des Rechts*, 1913, the translation of which was published by Harvard in 1936. Ehrlich was educated in Vienna and became professor of Roman Law in Czernowitz, which belonged to Austria until 1918 and to Rumania since then. It may not have been a coincidence that the first book on sociology of law was produced in a place which was a welter of nationalities, cultures, languages and laws. Though remarkably wide, however, Ehrlich's horizon was limited to Europe.

There is a great deal about law in the writings of evolutionist sociologists and anthropologists beginning with Herbert Spencer's *Principles of Sociology*. The last example of the kind is the erudite book by A.S. Diamond: *The Evolution of Law and Order*. The guiding idea in these works is to arrange legal codes in accordance with the degree of complexity and correspondence to broad economic categories like hunting-gathering, pastoralism, lower and higher agriculture, and so on. Comparisons are used to classify rather than to unravel causal relationships, as to a large extent is done by Weber. So, his sociology of law remains unique . . . which does not mean that it is faultless.

The conceptual apparatus of Weber's sociology of law is a good deal less impressive than its factual coverage. The confusing distinction between '*subjektive Recht*' and '*objektive Recht*' can be easily avoided in an English translation because English has two words 'law' and 'right', both of which are covered by German '*Recht*'. Nowhere does Weber explain what he means by 'objective' and 'subjective', but we can see that '*objektive Recht*' is simply English 'law' because in the text he says that '*objektive Recht*' in England consists of the Statute Law and the Common Law. From the examples of '*subjektive Recht*' it is equally evident that it means 'rights' in English. So, in English we can avoid the tenebrous terms 'subjective' and 'objective', full of metaphysical undertones, and the weird implication, entailed by Weber's usage, that 'subjective' is part of 'objective'.

Perhaps even more confusing is Weber's distinction between 'formal' and 'material'. On the top of this 'formal' and 'formalism' are used in different senses which leads him to contradict himself: in one sentence he says that 'formalism' is a part of 'rationalisation' of the law, while in another he says that 'formalism' impedes 'rationalisation' (see p. 468 of the first edition of *Wirtschaft und Gesellschaft*). To make sense out of what he is saying we must find clearer substitutes for his terms, which would correspond to the meaning which can be inferred from the common characteristics of the matters to which he applies his terms. When we do this we can see that when he speaks of decision-making on 'formal grounds' as opposed to 'material grounds' or 'material considerations', or of 'formal' as opposed to 'material' considerations, we can replace 'formal' by 'the letter of the law' or 'strict adherence to the letter of the law', while 'material' can be replaced by 'ethical considerations', 'moral justice' or equity. 'Formalism' in the sense of decision-making in accordance with the letter of the law makes the law 'rational' or 'rationalised', according to him, and a process leading to such a state of affairs constitutes 'rationalisation of the law'. In some passages, however, he uses 'formalism' interchangeably with 'ritualism', which leads him to contradict himself because he says that 'ritualism' is incompatible with 'rational' law. In the context of pronouncements to this effect he uses 'formalism' or 'ritualism' to denote procedures where decisive weight is attached to gestures or the way in which a sentence is pronounced rather than to its content. One of the examples he gives is the practice of the customary courts of the ancient Teutons who rejected evidence if the words conveying it were pronounced in the wrong order.

The foregoing semantic analysis enables us to see what Weber is getting at and why he attaches so much weight to it: he thinks that capitalism requires predictability of outcomes of legal arrangements which means regularity of procedures, which in turn requires some coherence of the norms and the stress on their meaning rather than inessential rituals which introduce a greater element of chance. That this is a correct interpretation can be seen from the following quotation and especially from the metaphor which he employs (p. 468 of the first edition of *Wirtschaft und Gesellschaft*):

> In so far as the specific legal formalism permits the legal machinery to function like a technically rational machine, it gives to every legal person a relative maximum of manouvering space for the freedom of movement and in particular for a rational calculation of legal consequences and likely outcomes of purposeful actions.

As usual Weber employs too many words, some of which are completely superfluous, but what he says is true: without regularity in legal procedures business transactions are sheer gamble.

There is another concept which must be explained. When talking about 'rationalisation', Weber also mentions 'systematisation' of the law. As usual he does not explain what he means by it or whether 'systematisation' is a part or aspect of 'rationalisation', although we can see that this is implied. We can also gather from the context that what he means by 'systematisation' is either codification or the effort on the part of the judges to make case law clear and free from contradictions. We can easily understand why Weber regards this as very important, as it is obvious that if the norms are completely ambiguous and contradictory, outcomes of legal transactions must be unpredictable. He errs, however, in implying, especially by some of his uses of the word 'rational', that the Roman law and the laws of the European states in the modern era are more precise and coherent than the laws and customs of other cultures. In fact anyone who reads what A.R. Radcliffe-Brown says about the Australian aborigines, whom he studied at the beginning of the present century, will see that the rules which govern their behaviour are no less precise and coherent than the laws of any industrial nation. Actually, they seem to be more precise and coherent, the reason being that they regulate societies which are smaller, simpler and stabler.

It is probably true that, as Weber says, the Roman jurists put more mental effort and rational thinking into producing a coherent body of laws than was ever done before. They had to do this to maintain order in a vast empire which incorporated a multitude of peoples with different laws, customs, religions and ways of life, while the social stratification was undergoing a transformation and the political and economic structures were becoming more complex. The task was greater but it does not follow that the product was distinguished by greater clarity and coherence than the laws of any of the conquered nations. In a stable and homogenous society the norms of conduct acquire precision and coherence through a spontaneous process of mutual adjustment without the need for conscious systematisation. There is an analogy here to what happens to a language. It is change – especially if it is rapid and in the direction of greater size, differentiation and interdependence – which calls for a greater conscious effort to maintain some degree of coherence between the norms, which none the less may be lower than in simpler societies. And a retrogression in respect of coherence may take place. I have the impression that the laws in Britain and the USA (and probably of a number of other countries) are less coherent, and the outcomes of legal procedures less predictable, than they were thirty years ago in consequence of the flood of legislation, diminished moral consensus, increased complexity of the economy and rapid social change.

Precision and coherence of the norms are necessary but not sufficient conditions of regularity of legal procedures because even very precise and non-contradictory norms may be subjected to arbitrary interference or simply broken. So let us look at the latter aspect of regularity to see whether we can find some justification in this respect for Weber's grading of legal systems by degrees of 'rationality'. As in connection with other semantic loads of this much abused word, Weber examines no evidence for his imputations of waywardness and fortuity to the legal norms and procedures of polities outside ancient Rome and modern western Europe. His error is the opposite of that of most students of primitive law at that time who on the whole agreed with Henry Sumner Maine that the primitive man is 'the slave of the custom'. Bronislaw Malinowski's *Crime and Custom in Savage Society* attracted much attention when it was published in the 1920s because it showed that the Trobriand islanders are not unlike so-called civilised people in not always complying with the norms which they acknowledge as valid. Many other field studies made since then have shown that tribesmen are neither as wild and law-less as Hobbes and many early writers imagined, nor such 'slaves of the custom' as the nineteenth-century evolutionists believed. In the light of anthropological literature the verdicts of African tribal courts and kings certainly do not appear haphazard. So, Weber was wrong about this.

Nor was he right about the unpredictability of legal procedures in Asiatic civilisations. In the seventeenth century the Ottoman empire was the best organised state in the world. There is no evidence that the verdicts of the Turkish courts were at that time less predictable than those of their counterparts in Christendom. By the eighteenth century there was more disorder and insecurity in the Ottoman empire than in the European monarchies, perhaps with the exception of Poland which was disintegrating. At the same time the Chinese empire was living through a period of order and stability, but although the population was growing rapidly, the methods of production and the forms of economy were unchanging. The legal procedures in China at the beginning of the nineteenth century do not appear more haphazard than in Britain where technical and economic progress was accelerating. It is likely that never was law more regularly administered than in Germany in Weber's days, but the situation in this respect was not radically different in Prussia of Frederick II which was very rural with very little capitalist development. What Weber tells us about Roman history invalidates his notion about 'rationalisation' going parallel in law and economy. Roman law, according to him, reached the height of 'rationalisation' in the codification during the reign of Justinian I. However, as he says many times elsewhere, Roman capitalism had withered two or three centuries earlier. It follows from his various statements (which, however, he does not connect) that in the course of Roman history capitalism flourished when the law was less 'rational', and decayed when the law was being 'rationalised'.

The most that can be saved from Weber's thesis about the connection between 'rational' law and 'rational' economy is that a high degree of regularity in legal procedures is a necessary condition of development of business enterprise or capitalism, if you prefer. It is clear, however, that it is not a sufficient condition because equally important is the content of the rules which are regularly followed and enforced: to permit capitalism to develop or even survive they must guarantee security of property and profit, allow the charging of interest, and give freedom to buy and sell goods, and to bargain about prices. If the laws restrict such activities, then the less regularly they are applied, the more room there will be for some capitalism. Although this was not true in the days of Stalin's terror, and does not apply to the constitution which is a mere façade, the legal procedures in the USSR are just as 'rational' by any of Weber's implicit criteria as anywhere else in the world. I would even say that they may be more 'rational' than in the West in recent years, as the norms which affect everyday lives of ordinary people seem to be more regularly and consistently enforced in the USSR. Nevertheless, they prevent development of capitalism because many of them have been deliberately designed for this purpose.

Much of the chapter (or of the book in the English version) deals with the factors which hinder 'rationalisation' of the law. But, since this concept is very shaky and used like an old flail, it is not surprising that the disquisition does not add up to much and is mostly circular, largely boiling down to reiterative rephrasing of the tautology that such and such legal framework is 'irrational' because it is not 'rational' and has not been 'rationalised'. In his works which I classify as historical sociology Weber makes interesting statements about how accumulation of capital through production and trade is hindered by such factors as predatory despotism, constricting bureaucracy, spoliatory and demagogue-ridden democracy, religious constraints on profit-seeking, investment, interest and bargaining, communality of property, ritual fixation of methods of production, and so on. He could have brought together and harmonised these insights in his systematic sociology. This he has not done, while in his sociology

91

of law he wants to find causes, if not the cause, in some feature of legal norms which is independent of their content. Beguiled by his treacherous notion of 'rationality', he gets into a blind alley of circular explanations.

It is a chastening lesson to see how a writer of genius gets bogged down by a faulty concept in the piece of work which displays the most astounding array of erudition. The reason is that he relied on dubious concepts most heavily precisely in the field where clarity is most necessary. Fortunately, despite the unfruitfulness of the main thesis, he says many interesting things about particular cases and circumstances, and throws sidelights which make his sociology of law well worth reading, provided it is treated as food for thought rather than a reliable end product.

4.2 Religion

Although sociology of religion looms so large on the title pages of Weber's works, what he says about it seems to me less impressive (especially in relation to the space which he devotes to it) than his treatment of politico-economic aspects of social structure. In section 3.3 I have already shown that his grading of religions on the scale of 'rationality' must be rejected as groundless: he repeatedly makes assertions to this effect but offers no arguments to support them beyond saying that Judaism and Christianity eliminated magic. The witch craze of the sixteenth and seventeenth centuries alone, to repeat, makes the idea of a 'rationalisation' or 'demagicalisation' of the view of the world at that time appear very far-fetched. The latter concept – Weber's '*Entzauberung*' – is translated by Talcott Parsons as 'disenchantment', which does not convey what Weber is getting at.

A general weakening of the beliefs in magic did not occur until the eighteenth century when scientific discoveries began to affect general mentality – in other words, in consequence of the rise of science, as many thinkers from Voltaire to Lecky rightly believed. Weber's originality consists in inverting this sequence and claiming that 'demagicalisation' preceded the rise of science and was a necessary condition thereof. He does not put it like this (and, as usual, is a bit vague about the exact sequence of cause and effect) but this view is clearly implied by what he says about 'demagicalisation' having preceded (or being part of) 'rationalisation', connected with the rise of 'rational' capitalism. The idea was new but is wrong. James Frazer was much nearer the truth when he said that magic was primitive science – the product of the quest for knowledge and power over the environment, pursued in the conditions which made wild errors inevitable and illusions of fictitious power irresistibly tempting. Research in the history of science has made it much clearer than it was in Weber's time that the separation (or distillation) of science from magic was a very slow and intermittent process which advanced unevenly in different fields. Very gradually science has been displacing magic, but it is arguable that in medicine (especially psychiatry) the process is not yet completed. The study of human behaviour (as I have shown in *Social Sciences as Sorcery*) still remains largely under the sway of magical thinking.

Weber completely misinterprets what he regards as 'hostility to magic' of the Hebrew prophets and rabbis and of the Christian churches. The prophets worked miracles and the priests (whether Israelite or Christian) performed rituals which were (and in most denominations still are) just as magical as anything done by those whom they lambasted as idolaters and sorcerers. The hostility of Judaism and Christianity to other religions stemmed not from any superior 'rationality' on either side but from competition between different groups of suppliers of occult aids for control over the souls. It is astonishing that Weber goes on about the contribution which Judaism (and especially its prophets) have made to 'the rationalisation' of culture while knowing very well that science and analytic philosophy were created entirely by the polytheistic Greeks without any Hebrews participating in it – a fact to which he pays no attention. The first Jews who made contributions to science belonged to the Islamic civilisation, while Copernicus was the first Christian who advanced beyond the ancient Greeks. Looking for the seeds of science in the content of Christian dogmas overlooks the coincidence between the spread of Christianity and general intellectual retrogression. Science began to develop more than a thousand years later and only in regions and periods where the preponderance of the priesthood was weakened in some measure.

Since the shortcomings of the notion of 'rationalisation' have already been indicated in an earlier chapter, I shall now turn to other aspects of Weber's systematic sociology of religion. Though based (like almost all Weber's writings) on an astounding array of historical information, this part of *Wirtschaft und Gesellschaft* (which appeared in English as a separate book) is not so unique on this score as his sociology of law because comparative study of religion attracted a larger number of men of extremely wide learning. Consequently in this field Weber had rivals equal, if not superior, in the range of factual information, such as James Frazer, Edward Westermarck or John Mackinnon Robertson. The least impressive is Weber's chapter on the origin and

93

development (*Entstehung*) of religions which seems decidedly inferior in ingenuity, persuasiveness and orderly marshalling of evidence to the treatment of this subject by Herbert Spencer or Edward Tylor.

More original is Weber's attempt to find links between forms of religiosity and social class, which none of the aforementioned writers made, and which is clearly inspired by Marx, Engels and probably Karl Kautsky whose book on *The Origin of Christianity* appeared in German in 1908. Weber, however, does not want to follow them in explaining a gravitation of a class towards a given form of religion by the latter's fitness to serve the economic interests of that class, although in his historical sociology – especially in his treatment of Hinduism and its role in domesticating the masses – he comes close to this viewpoint. In his systematic sociology he wavers and puts forth generalisations about typical traits of the religiosity of the artisans, merchants, peasants, and warriors. He does not restrict the applicability of his generalisations to a particular country or period and offers them as indications of cross-cultural tendencies. He illustrates them by examples of debatable correctness and does not even attempt to substantiate them by marshalling evidence. The truth is that historical data needed to justify such generalisations were not available to him and scarcely exist even now. It is all well worth reading as food for thought and a source of suggestions for research, but I have not found in Weber's systematic sociology of religion any generalisations which are well supported by data and highly likely to be true. Equally scarce in this work seem to be explanations of various turns in the history of religions of the kind that we find in his treatment of Judaism and which can be found in greater abundance in various works of John Mackinnon Robertson.

In my opinion, Weber's ideas on the influence of religion on the rise of capitalism are much more valuable than his systematic sociology of religion. It is an illuminating thought that autonomy of the cities in Christian Europe which was, as he correctly believed, a precondition of the rise of Western civilisation, was made possible by the insistence of the church on community of all faithful, which forestalled a ritualistic segregation among townsmen, thus permitting their joint action and eventual emancipation from the control by overlords. I am sure he is right about this as well as in seeing in Hindu caste barriers an insuperable obstacle on this road to municipal autonomy. I am equally sure, however, that he is wrong about China. In contrast to Christianity, according to him, the Chinese religion did not break the barriers between the clans which prevented the city dwellers from uniting to fight for autonomy. But China is the only part of the world which has experienced successful peasant uprisings which three times led to a displacement of the dynasty and a part of the mandarins by new rulers sprung from peasants. In Europe the only revolt of the poor which did not end by being drowned in blood was the uprising of the Ukrainian cossacks and peasants led by Bohdan Chmelnitzki in the seventeenth century; but they escaped a defeat by their Polish lords only by submitting to Moscow. Now, since (as Weber himself says) the clan barriers were at least as strong in villages as in towns, and yet did not prevent a unification of the Chinese peasants for collective action crowned with successes without parallel elsewhere, there is no reason to suppose that these barriers might have prevented the townsmen from uniting to fight for autonomy, had other circumstances been as favourable as in Europe. The most crucial of these circumstances was the feudal dispersion of power and the balance of power between the monarchy and the church which were unique and linked features of Western Christendom.

There are other examples which show that Weber somewhat overstated his case. Islam insisted at least as much as Christianity on the unity of the faithful and yet no city within its domains won a legal autonomy. It is true that Weber's thesis can be adapted to fit this case up to a point, but at the price of shifting the focus: as he points out in other contexts, many Islamic cities had populations consisting of Moslems, Christians and Jews. So an impediment to united action was there, however, not because of any lack of stress in Islam on unity of the faithful but because the Moslems were more tolerant and less eager than the Christians to offer the unbelievers a choice between conversion and expulsion or death, despite the Koranic command to spread the faith by the sword which stands in a stark contrast to the absolute pacifism of Jesus. The discrepancy between the dogma and the practice thus ran in opposite directions in the two religions. The explanation seems to be that the Islamic rulers had a fiscal interest in not forcing the non-believers to convert because the Koran exempts the Moslems from poll tax.

The absence of city autonomy in Byzantium and Russia shows that insistence on religious unity is not a sufficient condition thereof, as there was no difference on this point between the Eastern and Western Christianity. In the latter civilisation, moreover, city autonomy withered when feudalism gave place to absolutism. Poland constituted an exception to the pattern prevalent in Western Christendom: there the cities were sub-jugated by the landed nobility after they reduced the kings to impotence and began to favour the Jews who had to be docile as strangers. Thus the case of Poland fits Weber's thesis that religious divisions within cities make them unable to fight for autonomy.

Weber made here a very original, important and valid point which can be better defended against possible criticism by making clear that the factor which he has pointed out constitutes a necessary, though not a sufficient, condition of autonomy of the cities. Equally important is his famous thesis on the influence of Protestantism on the rise of capitalism (and therefore of the Western civilisation) which I examine in a later chapter. Both theses come under historical rather than systematic sociology, and they, rather than the latter, form parts of the basis of his title to greatness.

4.3 General comments on types of power

In Weber's systematic comparative sociology the parts devoted to the city and the types of power (*Herrschaft*) strike me as decidedly better than those which deal with sociology of religion and law. The comparative survey of the role of cities in various civilisations contains among other things the main elements of the explanation of why industrial capitalism rose in the modern Europe and nowhere else. It is a marvellous piece of writing, but I shall say no more about it here as Weber's views on the role of cities in history are discussed in chapter 5, section 4.

The comments about types of power or rule must begin with the question of how to translate '*Herrschaft*'. The current translation is 'authority', which has the defect that it suggests some measure of legality or legitimation, which '*Herrschaft*' does not. For this reason I prefer to translate it as 'rule', 'power' or 'domination' to make sure that no assumption about legitimacy is implied.

In view of the prevalence of misconception, it cannot be overemphasised that Weber's importance is not due to the excellence of his definitions of classifications. As we shall see in a moment, even the concept 'charisma' represents a merely terminological innovation and is neither defined nor used consistently. The only conceptual innovation consists of the misuse of the word 'rational' in the expression '*rationale Herrschaft*' which is usually translated as 'rational authority'. He certainly does not mean thereby 'rational exercise of authority or power' – which would be a perfectly defensible usage, provided the criteria were explained and illustrated. We can infer what he is getting at from the way he uses 'rational' and 'legal' as more or less interchangeable terms, sometimes lumping them together.

Furthermore, in the first, morphological, part of *Wirtschaft und Gesellschaft* he says that there are three types of legitimate power or domination (*Herrschaft*): traditional, charismatic and rational. This implies that 'rational' is an opposite of 'charismatic' or 'traditional' within the class of 'legitimate' domination or power – 'legitimate' in the sense of being regarded as such by those who obey. We can make better sense of what he says about power if we replace 'rational' in such contexts by 'legal'. So we would have power derived from formalised laws as opposed to one based on custom or personal magnetism (charisma) of the leader. Apart from the notorious difficulty of distinguishing between law and custom, this scheme has a much graver fault of making tacit assumption that what is legal is legitimate. This is unwarranted, as there are innumerable examples of laws which are obeyed solely out of fear of punishment rather than the sense of duty. True, Weber's definition does not strictly rule out the possibility of a law which is regarded as illegitimate by most of those to whom it applies, but it has no place in his classificatory scheme. This is a serious shortcoming because congruence (or incongruence) between laws and sentiments of duty and loyalty constitutes one of the most important determinants of how a society or group functions. Provided these shortcomings are avoided, there is nothing wrong in employing the expression 'legal power' or 'legal authority', although the latter is rather pleonastic because 'authority' implies legality. People speak about illegal power or rule but 'illegal authority' sounds incongruous.

There is nothing commendable about the lumping together of the words 'rational' and 'legal' in the expression 'legal-rational power'. As a concept it is worse than useless because (apart from the intrinsic faultiness of the second element) it insinuates that whatever is legal must be rational and vice versa. True, in strict logic this need not be so as in addition to power which is legal and rational we could have a type of power which is neither, or either one or the other but not both. So, if Weber wished to refrain from making the aforementioned gratuitous assumption, he ought to have said something about power which is legal but not rational, or rational but not legal, or illegal and irrational. It would be quite easy to think of examples which could plausibly be put into each box, if we were prepared to overlook the inappropriateness of applying the attribute 'rational' to power rather than the way in which it is exercised. We can get away from these conundrums by translating '*rationale Herrschaft*' as 'administrative authority', since it is fairly clear from the contexts in which this term appears that Weber has in mind power or domination exercised by, through or within an organised administrative hierarchy. Bearing this in mind, we can make sense out of what on the face of it looks like an unintelligent contradiction: in his systematic sociology Weber says that bureaucracy is a (if not the) rational type of domination, while in the political writings he goes on at considerable length about its inanities.

The list of Weber's types of power does not make a proper classification: it has no common criterion or criteria of division, and the classes are not mutually exclusive, nor do they exhaust the universe of discourse. On this score he is well below the level reached by Aristotle. When the latter proposed his classification of forms of government he employed two criteria (or principles of division, as he calls them): (1) the number of those who take part in governing – one, few, many; (2) the dichotomy between healthy and corrupt (or degenerate) forms; thus obtaining six types. There is nothing so neat in Weber. Even worse: some of the types are not defined at all. Thus in the long chapter on patrimonialism – an impressive piece of work, full of recondite factual information and valuable inductive approximations – he makes no attempt to explain what he means by it, which can only be inferred from the context.

Fortunately, inadequacy of definitions and classifications does not destroy the value of his insights into causation of historical process, although it does create the need for clarification and corrections. Even in physics a certain glossing over the lack of logical rigour has been necessary for progress. For example: the followers of Descartes refused to accept Newton's theories on the ground that the concepts of inertia and acceleration rested upon the concept of absolute space which they regarded as vacuous. Descartes taught that 'position' and 'movement' are relationships between things. This idea was revived by Einstein and constituted the starting point in the construction of the theory of relativity. However, historians and philosophers of science agree that the Cartesian vortex theory was a dead end, and that theory of relativity could only be conceived on the basis of Newtonian physics. If even in the most exact of the sciences unsatisfactory assumptions had to be accepted for the sake of explanatory power, how much more tolerant we must be in the inexact sciences. In other words, we must realise that insistence on perfect order at once may lead to sterility.

Despite inadequate logical rigour and clarity, Weber's classifications deserve attentive study because they offer the most comprehensive panorama of possible combinations of various structural characteristics of societies and groups.

4.4 Bureaucracy

Weber is often quoted as if he were the inventor of the concept of bureaucracy. This, of course, is completely untrue: the term was coined in France at the beginning of the nineteenth century and an entire book on this subject – *Die Burocratie* by Jozef Olszewski – appeared in 1904. The question is: what has Weber added and wherein lies its value?

As can be seen from Martin Albrow's excellent book on the history of this term – *Bureaucracy* (London, 1970) – Weber's definition stands aside from the other usages which are all pejorative. Chapter VI of Part III of the first edition of *Wirtschaft und Gesellschaft* has the heading 'Bureaucracy', but the opening sentence refers to 'officialdom'. It must be noted that German *'Beamtentum'* does not have the contemptuous undertones of English 'officialdom'. (It might be worth noting on the margin as a curiosity that while English is in the middle, Polish is at the opposite extreme from the German, as it has about eight derivatives from the Polish root for 'official' all of which are loaded with contempt.) Had the text been handed to the printer while Weber was still alive he could have been criticised for careless writing, as he replaces 'officialdom' by 'bureaucracy' in the middle of his definition. Anyway here are the essential points from it in my translation:

> The specific way in which modern officialdom functions finds its expression in the following features:
> 1. The principle of strict division of spheres of authority determined by general rules – laws and regulations. . . .
> 2. The principle of hierarchy of offices and the channelling of communication through proper hierarchic levels.
> 3. . . . the modern administrative organisation separates thoroughly official activities from private affairs.
> 4. The work of an official . . . requires thorough training.
> 5. Official duties are discharged in accordance . . . with general rules . . .

On the fourth page of this chapter Weber slips in the key word in an adjectival form when he thus describes the position of an official:

> 1. An official enjoys a high status . . .
> 2. An official of a purely bureaucratic type is appointed from above. An official elected by the ruled is no longer a purely bureaucratic figure.
> 3. There is . . . life long tenure.

4. An official receives a fixed salary and a retirement pension in money.

The only criticism that can be made here is under (2) that the reference to 'purely bureaucratic type' is superfluous. In English (and the same applies to German '*der Beamte*') the meaning of 'an official' entails appointment from above. Someone elected might be called 'an office-holder' but never 'an official'. Otherwise these statements are unobjectionable but can hardly be regarded as a great contribution to knowledge because they restate what was generally agreed. Contrary to what is often said, Weber's characterisation hardly constitutes an ideal type because it fits perfectly the civil and military services of all modern states. However, on a point which he adds later Weber is wrong. He says that 'when this type ['bureaucracy'] is fully developed, the official hierarchy is monocratically organised'. This can be made true by definition but then we would have to say that not only the civil services but also business management and even the armed forces have been becoming less fully developed or less bureaucratic, as the trend is undoubtedly away from monocracy and towards rule by committees.

As Weber's definition boils down to a list of the essential features of all centralised and well-organised administrative machines, I agree with his critics (for example E. Strauss in *The Ruling Servants*) who find it misleading to apply to every such machine the label 'bureaucracy' which was coined (and continues to be used) to pinpoint either the excessive power which the officials wield or various kinds of malfunctioning of the official bodies. Although any attempt to introduce a more consistent and clearer terminology is bound to be an uphill effort against a perennial tendency towards obfuscation inherent in the common usage of the terms which are very abstract and elusive as well as charged with political passions, we can hardly justify our claims to represent some kind of science unless we can use the words with a greater precision than the man in the street.

At the very minimum we ought to have four separate terms for the four clearly distinct meanings which are indiscriminately attached to the word 'bureaucracy'.

1 The set of people who perform the administrative functions in the manner described by Weber.

2 The network of the relationships in which they are enmeshed.

3 The amount of power which they wield as a body.

4 The various kinds of malfunctioning of the administrative machine.

There are various words which are available for the first

meaning: 'officials', 'functionaries', 'officialdom'. They do not, however, cover administrators who are not employees of the state. It was one of the chief contributions of Weber in this area that he clearly saw and emphasised the analogies between public and industrial administration although in those days the latter was almost entirely private. This perhaps, prompted him to redefine (and, in my opinion, over-extend) the concept of bureaucracy. Rather than use 'bureaucracy' in the corporeal sense, it is better to speak of 'the administrators' or the 'administrative class'. In a state with a private economy this class consists of two main sectors: business managers and state officials. When these are very powerful we could call them bureaucrats. Albrow thinks that the distinction between 'the bureaucracy' and 'bureaucracy' enables us to keep in mind the difference between a set of people and a form of government, but I fear that this may be cutting it a bit too fine. I feel it is less likely to lead to confusion to speak of the administrative class. There is nothing particularly strained in such a usage because we already commonly speak of public and business administration.

The second of the meanings of 'bureaucracy' distinguished above – the network of relationships in which the administrators are enmeshed at work – is unambiguously covered by such expressions as 'the administrative machine' or 'machinery' or 'the administrative hierarchy'.

In view of its etymology, 'bureaucracy' ought to be reserved for the third of the aforementioned meanings: the condition when the power of the administrators is greater than that of any other group of leaders or holders of authority: that is when they dominate the society. In this sense bureaucracy is clearly a matter of degree.

Weber did not live to see a complete or full bureaucracy in this sense because it materialised only with the depersonalisation of the government of the USSR after Stalin's death. Lenin was a charismatic leader of the revolution who invented and built a new political and economic machine which at the moment of his death was still governed by ex-revolutionary doctrinaires and orators. These were eliminated by Stalin who turned the USSR into a bureaucracy. But he was no regular official and so long as he lived the political structure was a mixture of personal dictatorship with bureaucracy. With the elimination of the former element, bureaucracy reached its fullness under Brezhnev who got to the top of the ladder by regular promotion as a capable and disciplined official.

Of all the pre-industrial states, the Chinese empire was the nearest to a full bureaucracy, as no other class could challenge the mandarins. Nevertheless, their power was incomplete because it was limited by the prerogative of the hereditary monarch and the influence of the emperor's relatives and favourites. The late Roman empire briefly reached an even higher degree of bureaucracy when the hereditary succession to the throne (never fully established) was set aside and the emperors nominated their successors. No pre-communist European state reached the degree of bureaucracy shown by the late Roman and Chinese empires. Everywhere in Europe the power of the officials was counterbalanced by that of the monarchs, their relatives, the landed nobility, the clergy; and later the politicians, the businessmen, the capitalists, the union leaders and the voters.

On this interpretation of 'bureaucracy', 'bureaucratisation' would mean the growth of the power of professional and regular administrators in relation to the other sectors of the population.

For the fourth meaning distinguished above – that is, various kinds of malfunctioning of the administrative machines – I have proposed in another book the term 'bureaupathy' which has the advantage that from it can be derived a name for a carrier of the tendency: 'a bureaupath'. The study of these tendencies might be called 'bureaupathology'.

It follows from what I have said about 'rationalisation' that 'efficiency' is also a relational attribute which is meaningless except in relation to a given goal. Its meaning is clearest when this goal is a measurable variable which is to be maximised. What is an efficient organisation for one purpose may be very inefficient for another. A dock may be inefficient at unloading ships but very efficient at providing the dockers with opportunities to make money by smuggling. None the less, excluding a sheer provision of sinecures, and assuming that an administrative machine is supposed to achieve some ascertainable effect upon the external world, we can specify the attributes which it must have to be able to carry out collective actions. Obversely (and more easily), we can list attributes which (if present in a sufficiently large dose) will incapacitate it for any kind of collective action. The examples are: apathy, laziness, incompetence, insubordination, bribery, nepotism, internal squabbles and intrigues, disregard of the regulations, failure to communicate, theft, vandalism, sabotage. However, when people fulminate about 'bureaucracy' they seldom have in mind any of the attitudes or actions listed above; and they usually refer to one or more of the following tendencies:

1 Proliferation of personnel far beyond what is needed for the declared task.

2   Multiplication of forms and formalities ('the red tape') which mainly or solely serve the purpose of providing employment for the superfluous personnel.

3   Avoidance of personal responsibility and decision, popularly known as 'passing the buck'.

4   Rigid and unthinking sticking to the letter of the regulations without regard or understanding of the purpose which they are supposed to serve.

5   Lack of checks on the power of the officials.

There is no reason to assume *a priori* that rule by officials must always be less desirable than other forms of domination. I do not even think that democracy must always be better than bureaucracy: the government of American cities by elected politicians has often been much more unjust and oppressive (not to speak of venality) than that of the departments of France by the prefects – regular civil servants appointed from Paris. The mandarins' rule of old China was on the whole better than that of the land-owning nobility in Poland. Speaking for a moment with less concern for precision (as this is not the place to expound in detail my political philosophy), I shall only say that (like Aristotle) I think that every form of government is susceptible to corruption (in the wide sense of the term) and is likely to be bad if pushed to the extreme. I also agree with the view (held in different forms by Polybius, Montesquieu and Gaetano Mosca) that the mixed or balanced government is the best; although even here I would add the proviso that the mixture may result in strife and paralysis rather than effective collective action if other factors prevent harmony in the body politic. I view the forms of government as having an instrumental rather than ultimate or intrinsic value. As the ultimate criterion of value I accept Bentham's postulate of the greatest happiness of the greatest number with the two provisos: (1) that the greater happiness of people is not obtained by inflicting greater suffering on animals; and (2) that happiness is not increased at the expense of human dignity and intelligence (which I regard as independent absolute values) by such means as drugging people to be contented idiots. I hope I shall be excused from having to define here what I mean by human dignity and intelligence, as the present remarks are only intended to show why I do not postulate that bureaucracy in any dose anywhere must be bad.

To come back to Weber, it appears that, apart from the unhelpful definition, he makes a mistaken empirical generalisation when he treats a rigid adherence to the regulations as a condition of efficiency. The more recent writers on public and industrial administration have pointed out that a very rigid adherence to the regulations tends to be counter-productive in relation to the goal which these regulations are supposed to promote. Actually, one of these writers – Marshall Dimmock – reserves the label 'bureaucracy' precisely for this attitude and contrasts it with efficient management which is only possible when the executives understand the general goal and are committed to it, understand how their particular tasks fit the general goal, and have some leeway in bending the regulations to the needs of unforeseen circumstances. I think that Dimmock is right, although I prefer the term 'formalism' to his use of 'bureaucracy'. Clearly, there can be no organisation without rules, but the capacity for collective action depends on optimisation rather than maximisation of rigidity. There is an analogy here with the bones which must neither be too soft nor too stiff.

In his political writings (as distinct from his general treatment of the concept) Weber comes near to recognising this point and criticises severely the workings of the German civil service and even uses 'bureaucracy' in the colloquial pejorative sense. He argues that the German state combines a great efficiency of execution with equally great stupidity of direction and attributes this state of affairs to the combination of an unintelligent hereditary monarch and the yes-men who got to the top through the process of selection which favoured unthinking obedience and toadying. He thought that the debates in the British parliament provided a better training for intelligent decision-making. So, he was not an adulator of the officialdom (as some of his recent critics would have us believe) although it is true that some of his statements lend themselves to this interpretation.

Enough has been said to show that here as in other contexts conceptual neatness was not Weber's strongest point and that it would be wrong to accept his definitions uncritically. Wherein, then, does his contribution to the study of bureaucracy (in any sense) lie? In the first place, in his awareness (much more original in his time than in ours) of the prevalence and importance of the phenomena covered by this term. In his historical and comparative studies, as well as in the comments on contemporary affairs, he always looks at the functions, status and power of the officials, their recruitment, training, remuneration and ethos. His general treatment of 'bureaucracy' remains unrivalled as a widely comparative survey of development of administrative machines, and of conditions and effects of this development. Although it has been common knowledge for a long time that China was ruled by the mandarins, Weber's volume on China was the first attempt to investigate the nature of this class in relation to other aspects of the Chinese society and its genesis. Though nominally devoted to the religion, the volume is much less original and of enduring value in its treatment thereof. In contrast, on the problems of bureaucracy and economy it remained completely unrivalled for several decades until it drew the attention of the sinologists to these questions. A number of them acknowledge their indebtedness to Weber. Much the same can be said about the volume on India.

As in medicine, an early diagnosis demands a great skill while a late one is usually very much easier. One needs no great perspicacity to realise today that the advance of bureaucracy is one of the key factors in social changes, but this was not so obvious at the end of the last century when free enterprise economy appeared in full bloom while not only ordinary people but also most political thinkers expected a steady progress towards democracy and liberty rather than an increase in the power of the officialdom. The forecasts of inevitable bureaucratisation made by Weber at that time must rank among the most correct sociological predications ever made. Of particular significance was his recognition of the privately owned free business enterprise as the chief promoter of bureaucratisation. He thought that discipline indispensable in the factory precluded socialism in any sense that would be acceptable to the founders of this ideology.

On this point Weber was immensely superior to Marx and Engels, whose most important errors stem from their failure to recognise the growing importance of the administrative functions and of the administrative class. This failure underlies their total inability to foresee the problem of putting socialism into practice, as well as their mistaken predictions about the future evolution of capitalism. The latter included the belief that the middle class will disappear and the society will be polarised into a small number of immensely rich capitalists and the rest consisting of miserable proletarians. The predictions about the growing misery of the proletariat were not unreasonable as extrapolations of the trend witnessed in the British Isles during the 'hungry forties'; but (fortunately for the proletariat) this trend was reversed soon after these prophecies were made, owing to the growth of wealth, mainly resulting from technical progress, later coupled with the spread of birth control, the development of the labour unions and the advance towards democracy. All these factors were disregarded by Marx and Engels because, it seems, their recognition would spoil the neatness of their scheme and the certainty about the coming revolution. The prediction about the disappearance of the middle class was based on their 'law of industrial concentration' – which was a very good generalisation and perhaps their greatest intellectual achievement, although they had a pre-decessor on this point in Simonde de Sismondi. Nevertheless, the predicted impact of this concentration on the class structure did not materialise; firstly because the advent of corporate enterprise permitted concentration of production without an equal concen-tration of ownership, and secondly because of the tremendous increase of the administrative personnel inside private firms as well as in the machinery of the state. The middle class which Marx and Engels knew in England (especially when they were young) – which consisted of small merchants and independent craftsmen – has indeed sunk into insignificance, as they predicted, but it was replaced by a much larger class of white-collar employees.

Writing several decades later – when the expression 'the new middle class' had already been made current in Germany by Emil Lederer – Weber could hardly make the same mistakes. In his pessimistic rather than Utopian view of the future, socialism as well as capitalism inevitably leads to bureaucracy.

If we look at the totality of his works we get a slightly ambiguous picture: in some passages (like these quoted below) he views bureaucratisation as inevitable, while in his political writings he suggests the ways in which it could be mitigated.

In his work on the evolution of social and economic systems of antiquity (published in 1909) he writes:

> constriction of private economic initiative by the bureaucracy is nothing specific to the Antiquity. . . . Every bureaucracy has the tendency to produce the same effects through its expan-sion. . . . This is true of ours too. . . . Today capitalism is the pace-maker of bureaucratisation of the economy. . . . As in Antiquity the bureaucratisation of society will (in all likeli-hood) eventually subdue capitalism.

In a lecture given in 1918 about socialism he says; 'what is advancing is not the dictatorship of the workers but of the officials'. Little has happened since to disprove his forecasts. True, he did not foresee what I call the flaccidation of administrative machines – the decline of discipline and actual central control – which has recently accompanied their numerical growth and the extension of the sphere of authority; and which in Britain, for example, has produced a combination of interven-tionism without real control, let alone planning. This, however, may be a transient phenomenon: a phase in the eternal political cycle envisaged by the ancient Greek philosophers when disorder leads to tyranny. So, Weber might have been right after all. On the other hand, it is equally possible that, if an ecological catastrophe is avoided through scientific progress and successful social adaptation, the bureaucracy of the future may be somewhat softer and rely more on manipulation rather than direct command than was the case in Weber's time. Anyway, no matter which way the trends will turn, there is little chance that Weber's thesis about the inevitability of bureaucratisation will lose its topicality.

4.5 Charisma

It has been said that Weber's sociology of religion was his answer to Marx and Nietzsche. There can be little doubt that this is true as far as Marx was concerned. Weber knew his writings and speaks of the works of Marx and Engels as 'a great achievement'. I have already said something about how Weber corrects or supplements Marx, but let us glance at the influence of Nietzsche. The indebtedness here is much less clear except in so far as Nietzsche's focus on the subtleties and perversities of human psyche constitutes an antidote to the one-sided and simplistic psychology which underlies the so-called materialist interpretation of history. However, the only definite idea which can plausibly be traced to Nietzsche's influence is Weber's concept of 'charisma'.

Though often treated as a pass-word to the temple of sociological knowledge, the concept of charisma is, in my opinion, one of the less valuable of Weber's contributions as it boils down to little more than a verbal innovation: a new label (taken from theology where it means a special gift bestowed by God) for the well-known fact that there are individuals who possess an extraordinary talent for imposing themselves as leaders and eliciting voluntary obedience. The appreciation of the personal element in history was not new: it was the common habit among the historians to attribute the turns of history to actions of great men; and, having read Nietzsche, Weber was acquainted with his vaguely theoretical musings on this topic. To forestall these remarks being taken as aspersions, I must stress that nowhere does Weber claim to have discovered this phenomenon. No doubt because it was so unimportant, this is the only one of Weber's innovations which has come down to the mass media and common parlance: I have even seen motorcycles advertised as having 'charisma'.

Although (as always) he says many interesting things in this context, it cannot be said that he clarifies the question of the personal element in leadership and authority because he uses the term 'charisma' in a contradictory manner. However, to be fair, we must bear in mind that his general treatment of this concept in *Wirtschaft und Gesellschaft* was never completed and was published posthumously, while the other volumes where he uses it were written some years earlier at considerable intervals. No matter how excusable, however, the contradictions remain. Having described it as the ability to inspire faith, loyalty and obedience, which is not derived from the laws or customs, and therefore forms the opposite of institutionalised authority, Weber sees in 'charisma' an agency which produces radical innovations in the institutions and established beliefs. Then (with his usual wealth of insights and magnificent comparative sweep) he proceeds to examine the transformations of 'charisma', showing how it inevitably undergoes 'a routinisation' and transforms itself into an established authority.

His prime example is Mohammed: a lone rebel and preacher, who gathers followers through his powers of persuasion and leadership, wins against odds because of his extraordinary talents, and finally becomes the founder of a new religion and a ruler of an empire. The transformation of a community of zealots into an orderly state was accompanied by 'the routinisation of the charisma'. Thus, if we want to be logical we must say that at some point during this process 'charisma' vanishes and is replaced by traditionally sanctioned aura of institutionalised authority. Weber in contrast speaks of 'hereditary charisma', 'royal charisma' and 'clan charisma', thus contravening his own statement of what the term is supposed to mean. Used so indiscriminately, this word becomes a superfluous substitute for 'aura', 'prestige', 'elevated status' or 'authority'. 'Charisma' is worth retaining as an analytic term only if we stick to the narrower conception. A charismatic leader, therefore, is one who has no organised 'machine' at his disposal, whose power has not been obtained through institutionalised procedure, and who converts people to his message and secures their obedience by persuasion. The founders of doctrinal communities satisfied these criteria perfectly so long as they had acquired neither an apparatus of coercion nor wealth. Jesus, for example, was a purely charismatic leader. So was John Wesley, Mohammed until he had organised an army, Gandhi before he acquired the backing of the party machine, and Lenin before he seized power in Russia. The opposite of a charismatic leader is a tyrant who rules through naked force and the fear which he inspires, or a ruler who is obeyed regardless of his personal capabilities and solely in virtue of the office which he holds.

As Weber pointed out, leadership can remain purely charismatic only so long as the number of the followers is small, that is to say at the very beginning of a successful movement, because the creation of an administrative machine and the acquisition of funds open possibilities of commanding men by applying coercion as well as by providing financial inducements. Moreover, the mere duration of the hierarchy inculcates the habits of obedience to the office, which soon acquire a force of inertia independent of the personal qualities of the holder. A transformation of a charismatic into an institutionalised leadership is usually called its routinisation, although 'adulteration' or 'dilution' might be a more illuminating term.

With the exception of the founders of small sects, enduring power can only be partially charismatic, that is, the leader's charisma can constitute only one of the props of his power. For many of his admirers, de Gaulle had a great deal of charisma, but he also had a police force and the entire apparatus of the state at his disposal to enforce his commands. As the bloody purge in 1934 has shown, Hitler could not rely on his charisma alone, even in his relations with the party stalwarts. Nevertheless, his power over most of the Germans had a very large (though varying) charismatic element, although his power over the conquered nations and his political opponents was based on naked force.

The term 'charisma' becomes superfluous and confusing if it is indiscriminately applied, as commonly happens, to such desperate phemonena as any kind of aura surrounding an office, the supernatural powers attributed to kings and priests, or even simple prestige or status: the expression 'routinisation' of charisma then becomes meaningless.

Even if used with sufficient rigour, the term 'charisma' can be of use only with reference to one aspect of the general problem of importance of individuals in determining 'great' events; because there are good arguments for the view that follies and vices of individuals in key positions have played just as important a role in determining 'the turns of history' as the appearance of 'great men'. This question is related to an even wider problem of the role of accidents in determining historical processes, which is sometimes discussed under the heading of 'the question of Cleopatra's nose' – the point being that if her nose had been less comely, she would not have been able to influence Caesar and Antony, and the history of Rome (and therefore of the world) would have been different. It has also been argued plausibly that had a genetic accident placed a more capable ruler on the throne of Louis XVI or Nicholas II, neither the French nor the Russian revolution would have occurred. Indeed, the first accident might have sufficed, because it is difficult to imagine how the Russian revolution (as we know it) could have occurred without having been preceded by the French. It is equally possible that had Henry VIII not caught syphilis and had he produced a son who would have been just as capable a tyrant as himself, no parliamentary system of government would have developed in England and therefore no industrial revolution would have taken place. Or would there be any communist regimes today had Lenin been shot before he had led the Bolsheviks to victory? On the other hand, it seems certain that big corporations would have developed in America if John D. Rockefeller, Andrew Carnegie and Cornelius Vanderbilt had died as children. Nor does it seem likely that democracy would have collapsed in Britain had any of the Prime Ministers been killed in an accident.

Although the fashion has now swung the other way, many deeply traditionalist historians still depict the events as purely haphazard outcomes of free decisions by great men. On the other side there are people whom Karl Popper calls (rather misleadingly) 'the historicists', and whom I prefer to call 'the predestinarians', who view history as a predetermined unfolding of an inevitable sequence. Weber held neither of these preconceptions and stood on the middle ground (but on a higher plane in terms of sophistication) between the hero-worshipping exaggerations of Carlyle and Nietzsche, and the equally unsound predestinarian oversimplification of Marx and Engels.

4.6 Feudalism and patrimonialism

Next to his treatment of the cities, the chapters devoted to feudalism and patrimonialism are, in my opinion, the most masterful of Weber's writings. Unlike his much more famous treatment of bureaucracy, they are not marred by the misleading concept of rationalisation which is rarely mentioned here. Furthermore, more than anywhere else Weber makes use here of his idea of ideal type, taking the classic Franco-German feudalism of the later Middle Ages as the extreme case in relation to which many other political formations can be arranged according to the degree of resemblance or divergence in various respects. Although a number of earlier writers (notably Marx and Engels) used this term in a wide sense and applied it to other civilisations, Weber's was the first systematic analysis of 'feudalism' as a generic concept in the light of comparative study of universal history. The problem of whether there was feudalism outside Europe (or even north-western Europe) has been debated before him, but Weber seems to have been the first to realise (or at least to make clear) that it was not a yes or no question – nor even a simple matter of degree – but that the features which are regarded as the essential characteristics of western Europe in feudalism, appear in various incomplete combinations in other parts of the world. As I have tried to show in the relevant passages of *Uses of Comparative Sociology*, 'feudalism' is employed in at least a dozen different senses, with the corresponding divergent denotations. If we define 'feudalism' as a system where a warrior nobility rules the peasantry, we shall find feudalism in most pre-industrial, supra-tribal societies. On the other hand, if we postulate that the entire hierarchy of government must be based on formal, bilaterally binding contracts of enfeoffment, then only France and Germany around 1200 satisfy this criterion. In contrast, the rewarding of officials and warriors by grants of land tilled by peasants is a very common arrangement: indeed practically universal in the states without developed currency. To distinguish between a system based on proper contracts and one where a grant of land can be revoked at the sovereign's pleasure, Weber introduces the terms 'fief feudalism' (*Lehenfeudalismus*) and 'benefice feudalism' (*Pfruendenfeudalismus*). Much of the text discusses oscillations along this continuum, their connection with the processes of dispersion or concentration of power, and causes and consequences thereof.

Even more far-ranging in time and space is the treatment of 'patrimonialism', perhaps because this is the most common form of government in history. A conceptual analysis, however, is lacking here and the concept is not even defined. It can be inferred from the examples that Weber has in mind the type of polity where there are no institutional limitations on the power of the monarch, who treats the territory and the population as his property and governs through his personal servants. Leaving aside polities governed by assemblies (that is where the people or at least the upper class collectively participated in governing) – examples of which can be found only in Graeco-Roman and western Christian civilisations, and which Weber discusses in 'City' – the pre-industrial states consisted of different mixtures of the elements of patrimonialism, feudalism and bureaucracy. Thus, most of universal history can be viewed as variations in relative doses of these ingredients. Weber does not put it quite like this, but this view can be distilled as the quintessence of what he says about these types of domination.

Patriarchalism appears as the primeval form of rule which (presumably through the growth in size) becomes patrimonialism. Bureaucracy develops within patrimonialism when the king's servants become numerous and organised into a disciplined and articulated (or, as Weber calls it, 'rational') hierarchy. On the

111

other hand, if the servants acquire some independence from the ruler, manage to limit his power, and establish contractual or semi-contractual relations with him, patrimonialism changes into feudalism. The latter can be transformed into a patrimonial bureaucracy or bureaucratic patrimonialism through a process of concentration of power and the growth of the administrative machine. This process, however, is not irreversible as dispersion of power within a primitive bureaucracy can lead to feudalism. These seem to be the barest bones of Weber's kaleidoscopic panorama of the interplay between the social forces which push societies towards one or the other of the types of domination. As far as the factual material used for comparative reasoning is concerned, Weber and Spencer are complementary: Weber knew history much better than ethnography, whereas with Spencer it was the other way round.

Weber also discusses domination by priests which he calls hierocracy. He was very far from being the first to pay attention to the political importance of priesthoods, and as usual his chief contribution lies in how he explains various evolutionary turns in history. From a more general viewpoint, the chief merit of the chapter 'State and Hierocracy' lies in never losing sight of the economic factors involved in the interplay between these elements, without falling into one-sided economic determinism.

In the light of Weber's writings we can view most states recorded by history as mixtures of patrimonialism, hierocracy, feudalism and bureaucracy, while the normal pattern of history appears as reversible changes in the relative weight of these ingredients. There have been two chief deviations from this normal pattern. One was political: the emergence of constitutional government by assemblies – first in Greece and Rome and later in Western Christendom. The other was the rise of scientific and industrial civilisation in the modern West which Weber equates with the rise of capitalism. He never desists from searching for causal connections which might help to explain these great deviations from the normal pattern of human history. Statements referring to these questions are strewn even throughout the most abstractly general discussions. Even when he seems to be engaged in pure classifying (if not cataloguing), he inserts remarks on this theme. Of course, he tries to explain many other things as well. To an even greater extent than the other parts of his systematic comparative sociology, the treatment of types of domination is marked by a search for explanations. Most of these explanatory sketches and suggestions are half-formulated and often merely implied, but this adds to their value as food for thought. Anyone in search of a good topic for an analysis of social causation can find it by formulating (and then examining) a tacitly assumed major premise in one of Weber's explanatory sketches.

5 Historical comparative sociology: the explanation of the rise of capitalism

5.1 Analysis and historical research

Judged by the quantity of historical material (including primary sources) which he digested, Weber ranks as a great historian. However, at least in his later years he studied history mainly in order to make comparisons. His case studies are strewn with references to other situations, explanations and generalisations. When writing about the prophets of ancient Israel, he presents a theory about the relations between peasants and town traders and usurers, about the bureaucratic state, and about how social protest of the peasants tends to be connected with movements for religious reform.

Weber was not the first to resort to comparisons in order to arrive at generalisations. Indeed, all the thinkers who have left their mark on the history of sociology did precisely that. Aristotle, Ibn-Khaldun, Bodin, Machiavelli, Montesquieu, Buckle, Spencer, Pareto, Mosca and many others – they all used comparative method. The moral of this, incidentally, is that the aspirants to Weber's mantle should postpone their attempts to produce another *Economy and Society* until they acquire a comparable range of factual information. Weber's achievement shows, moreover, that the knowledge of other societies, and the consequent ability to compare, aids enormously the analysis of any given society, and particularly the discovery of causal relationships.

To appreciate the magnitude of Weber's achievement, it must be remembered that when he prepared his *Religionssoziologie* next to nothing was known about social and economic history of China. He extracted his information on the structure of the Chinese society and its development from translated dynastic chronicles, reports of travellers and the pages of the *Peking Gazette*: a periodical in English published for foreign business-men in the days of extra-territorial 'concessions'. The amount of effort and perspicacity necessary for this task must have been prodigious. The same is true of his treatment of India. In the case of ancient Israel his task was somewhat lighter because the subject had been better studied; and so the factual mistakes appear to be fewer. The history of the economic and political institutions of the ancient Mediterranean world had been studied intensively even before Weber was born, and his contemporary Eduard Meyer attempted a synthesis in a remarkable essay on 'Economic Development in Antiquity'. During the sixty years since the appearance of *Agrarverhaeltnisse in Altertum*, many excellent works appeared in this field, the most comprehensive being those of Roztovzeff and Heichelheim. Nevertheless, Weber's sociological history, concealed under the modest title, remains unique. For it is neither an economic history (as it is commonly understood), nor a political nor a military, but a truly structural history, which shows how the economic changes influenced religion, how the innovations in tactics brought about the transformations of social stratification, how the distribution of political power impeded the growth of capitalism, and so on. All the time he tries to trace dynamic relations between various aspects of social life. His treatment of historical data is just as 'functionalist' as Malinowski's analyses of the Trobriand society; and in its light, the dispute between the functionalist and the historical schools of anthropology, which raged in the 1920s and 1930s, appears puerile.

Nobody who glances through any of his major works can fail to be impressed by the astounding array of detailed information. True, the same can be said about writers like Frazer, Ratzel, Westermarck, Spengler and Toynbee, but there is a great difference between them and Weber. In the first place, they had much less to say in the way of theoretical generalisation. Frazer and Westermarck were interested in establishing a sequence of evolutionary stages, and Ratzel in showing the influence of geographical environment. Actually their works constitute useful encyclopedias of customs, beliefs, and institutions. Toynbee has a theory but it is vague, tautological and unverifiable. The theory of challenge and response, for instance, is purely tautological. We are told that a civilisation develops when it responds successfully to a challenge; but how do we know that it has responded successfully, except by seeing that it has developed? Toynbee provides no criteria for an independent assessment of the two variables. *The Study of History* has considerable value, but chiefly as a source-book of recondite pieces of information. Whilst Frazer and Westermarck catalogued customs, and Spengler filled his books with spurious analogies between superficial features of mostly fictitious entities, Weber compared social structures and their functioning, noting differences as carefully as resemblances, and trying to relate isolated features to their structural contexts. When information on the structure of the society in which he was interested was lacking, he made truly Herculean efforts to extract it from the sources. Each volume of his *Religionssoziologie* would merit praise even if it were the single product of life-long work. In spite of many serious errors, the parts devoted to China and India still stand unrivalled as 'holistic' (or if you like, functionalist) analyses of these societies from a comparative viewpoint, revealing their inner springs, and showing the mutual dependence of various features of culture and society. His superiority over his most distinguished predecessors was largely due to the progress of historiography. Montesquieu could not have used similar data because they just were not available.

As judged from the vantage point of the present knowledge, Weber's errors of historical interpretation are mainly due to the difference between the data available to him and to us. Consequently they loom largest in his treatment of China because in this field the progress in structural history has been the fastest. Not only in Weber's time, but even as late as the 1940s there were no books on the social, economic or institutional history of China. The first general sketch of this kind was produced by Helmut Wilhelm in China occupied by the Japanese and published in German in Peking in 1944. When I began my comparative studies just after the war, I could find only the books by Marcel Granet and Henri Maspéro on the very ancient times, a book by an author whose name I cannot recall called an *Economic History of China* but which is in fact a translation of a chronicle, an article by Otto Franke on Wang An Shih's reforms, and three articles by Balasz on the Tang period which were the first thorough study of Chinese economic history, apart from a book on the economic system before the collapse of the empire, based on European sources only, written by Karl A. Wittfogel shortly before he had to flee from Hitler. The first sociologically oriented general history of China was written by Wolfram Eberhard in Turkey and first published in Turkish. The German edition appeared in 1948. All the German authors mentioned above had read Weber and acknowledge their debt to him with the exception of Wittfogel who was then a Marxist. Both French authors mentioned above had contacts with Emile Durkheim, and Granet was associated with the activities of the latter's school. Stimulated by the influx of refugees from China into the American universities after 1950, as well as by the development of research in Japan, the study of China's history – especially of the questions of its social structure – has progressed so much that now only a fool would try to reconstruct the past on the basis of slender data of the kind which Weber used.

Given the limitations under which he laboured, it is not in the least surprising that often Weber did not get it quite right, and we can only marvel at how he managed to hit the bull's eye on a number of crucial points. A stricture commonly made by specialists is that his picture is too static – as if the Chinese society did not change in the course of the two millennia. This is valid, but it is difficult to see how Weber could have avoided it when he was piecing together gleanings from ancient chronicles with recent reports from missionaries, without having much material for the intermediary period. On some points, however, the pendulum of criticism has swung in the opposite direction: it used to be said that recruitment into civil service through examinations dates only from the Sung period and that Weber extrapolated it too far back. However, in a fairly recent article on 'The Origins of Bureaucracy in China', H.G. Creel argues that it goes even further back than Weber supposed.

Weber himself – Creel writes –

acknowledged not only that he was not a Sinologist but that he did not even have the advice of one. In publishing his principal study of Chinese culture he wrote that he did so 'with misgivings and with the greatest reservation'. This awareness of his limitations did not, however, restrain Weber from attempting to make highly original interpretations of Chinese texts, producing results that are sometimes plainly contrary to fact. Another complication for which Weber is, of course, in no way to blame is the fact that much of the most important research on early China has been done since Weber died in 1920. Yet despite all these handicaps, his almost incredible genius produced, even in this field, some insights of great usefulness and uncanny accuracy. For these we can only be grateful. But these contributions, and Weber's well deserved reputation, should not blind us to the fact that in important respects Weber's picture of Chinese bureaucracy is a very misleading one. Thus (*The Religion of China*, 232) he tells us that in the Chinese character there is 'the absence of an inward core, of a unified way of life flowing from some central and autonomous value position'. Again Weber tells us that the

117

Confucian 'way of life could not allow a man an inward aspiration toward a "unified personality"'. But surely few ways of life, anywhere, have been so characterised as the Confucian by 'an inward striving toward a "unified personality"'. One wonders where Weber could have acquired such ideas. He prefaces these remarks by stating that for information concerning the Chinese character 'the sociologist essentially depends upon the literature of the missionaries'. It would be a little hard on 'the missionaries', however, to give them all the credit. In interpreting some passages in the *Analects*, Weber seems to have paid singularly little attention to the judgments of James Legge, a very great missionary scholar. Weber appears to have been unfortunate in selecting which missionaries to believe.

The defects of Weber's treatment of Chinese bureaucracy are those that we should expect when a master of brilliant generalisation, possessing inadequate and inaccurate information, attempts to reduce to tidy formulae a range of phenomena that resists generalisation. An example is the manner in which he uses the term 'literati'. He tells us (*The Religion of China*, 42) that the literati were 'ritualist advisers' of the princes and that 'the literati' of the feudal period . . . were first of all proficient in ritualism. He also informs us that Shang Yang was 'a representative of the literati', whereas Shang Yang was very far indeed from being a 'ritualist'. Again, he says 'if one may trust the Annals, the literati, being adherents of the bureaucratic organisation of the state as a compulsory institution, were opponents of feudalism from the very beginning'. This is confused and confusing. No matter how we define 'literati', whether we limit it to 'Confucians' or make it more inclusive, the men it must denote include individuals and groups whose attitudes on these matters were various and conflicting. . . .

Weber . . . was no Sinologist, and even Sinologists in his day hardly appreciated the degree to which bureaucratic techniques and regulations were elaborated in early China. Today, when information about them is gradually becoming more available, the facts are sometimes difficult to credit. Karl Bünger, 'Die Rechtsidee in der chinesischen Geschichte,' in *Saeculum III* (1952), writes that whereas in the Roman Empire administrative law was little developed, China had already at an early date a body of legal regulations for the administration of the state of astonishing completeness (H.G. Creel, *What is Taoism?*, University of Chicago Press, 1970).

Being famous for its inclination towards mysticism and complicated taboos, the Indian civilisation could more easily be shown as averse to 'rationality', and for this reason Weber's scheme of classifying civilisations along this dimension has led to fewer mistakes in his treatment of India. Furthermore, as the historical study of India has progressed much less since his time than that of China, there is less difference between secondary sources which Weber used and what is available to us, and consequently, his account and especially his explanatory interpretations have been superseded only on a few minor points. Not only in virtue of the comparative and theoretical insights, but also as a synthetic view of the nature and evolution of Indian society and culture, Weber's volume is richer than even such a recent and remarkable effort in this direction as D.D. Kosambi's *An Introduction to the Study of Indian History* (Bombay, 1966). In contrast to the volume on China, Weber's treatment of India cannot be criticised for being static. On the contrary, it is more dynamic – in the sense of dealing with institutional changes and the forces which produced them – than any other book available today, let alone in his lifetime. It is, among other things, the only explanatory account of the caste system which goes beyond the usual perspective limited to the factors of religion and the Aryan conquest, and puts it in relation to the economy and the structure of power. It also provides the most 'structural' and dynamic treatment of the rise and decline of Buddhism and Jainism. To repeat, Weber had a better starting point here than in his study of China. The institution of caste seemed to the Europeans so peculiar that it early attracted a good deal of attention, particularly as the contacts with India were much closer than with China. So, even in Weber's times there was a considerable literature on the institutional aspects of Indian history.

To my mind, his volume on India constitutes Weber's greatest achievement of historical interpretation. The volume on Judaism was easier to write because the secondary works were much better and the primary sources more easily accessible. The same is true of his study of classical antiquity. His interpretations of the latter are, therefore, less open to criticism on the score of factual errors. But for the same reason (though undoubtedly great works of synthesis, explanation and theory) they seem to me to constitute a lesser historiographic achievement than his reconstruction of India's evolution from much scantier sources.

5.2 Predatory *versus* productive capitalism

Weber's focus on 'capitalism' brings him closer to Marx than to

119

any other of his great forerunners. As neither was a clear and careful writer, they provide plenty of scope for figuring out what they 'really' meant. The works of Marx contain many contradictions not only because he changed his mind on many points in the course of his life, but also in consequence of the tension and oscillation between his two roles: of an erudite scholar and glib-tongued propagandist. In *The Communist Manifesto* Marx and Engels expound unilinear and predestinarian evolutionism coupled with simple technological determinism, according to which feudalism was produced by the water-mill and capitalism by the steam engine. None the less, they are not prepared to wait for another technical invention to produce socialism, but contradict their economic determinism by calling upon the workers to use the political means to bring it about. Even in their more scholarly works they often resort to teleological explanations of the crude kind commensurate with their predestinarian dogma, when for example they explain the English revolution on the ground that it was 'necessary' for the development of capitalism which they assume to have been pre-destined to develop. (This 'explanation' is reiterated even in the most recent literature; among others by the well-known Oxford historian Christopher Hill.) However, in some parts of *Das Kapital* and of *Die Grundrisse*, as well as in the fragments about the Asiatic 'mode of production', Marx deals with the causes or preconditions of the rise of capitalism. One of them, in his view, was the emergence of a class of workers who did not own the means of production, and therefore had to sell their labour. This was brought about through the expropriation of the peasants through enclosures. The other precondition of the rise of capitalism was, according to Marx, the emergence of a class of people who had enough money to buy labour. This happened in consequence of what he calls 'the primitive accumulation of capital', through land rents, trading mixed with piracy, booty from conquests and extraction of the gold and silver from America.

There is no doubt that the processes which Marx labels 'the primitive accumulation' did take place, but he was wrong about their consequences, and committed the error of explaining something very specific (i.e. the new mode of production which emerged first in Britain) by something much more common: namely appropriation and accumulation of wealth through coercion. Though very sad, the fate of the workers during the Industrial Revolution was not worse than that of the poor in many pre-industrial societies. The serfs who had to pull barges up the Volga, the Chinese rickshaw boys or sedan chair porters, the miners of gold or silver in Spanish Peru – not to speak of the

Roman galley slaves permanently chained to the oars – did not have a better life than the Lancashire mill hands. If 'primitive accumulation' were the crucial factor, an industrial revolution would have occurred long ago in ancient Rome or even Egypt; and if for some reason it were delayed until the modern times it would have occurred not in England but in Spain which was stuffed with the gold and silver from the Americas. Max Weber clearly saw this. And here we come to one of the fundamental insights: his distinction between 'rational' (i.e. industrial) capitalism and the 'irrational' (which he also calls 'booty', 'usury' or 'political' capitalism) was linked to the view that the latter was common (we could say perhaps, 'natural') whereas the former was exceptional; and therefore its appearance demands an explanation. In other words, to explain the rise of industrial capitalism (which, to repeat, Weber calls either 'rational' or 'modern'), we must discover the factors which have induced people who had money, first to save rather than spend it on ostentation, and then to invest it in developing production rather than in some form of spoliation. His prime example of political (or we should say, predatory) capitalism is the Roman tax farmers who not only did nothing to develop production but ruined entire provinces by their extortions.

Much evidence can be added to show that Weber was right while Marx was wrong, and that 'primitive accumulation' explains nothing. I have already mentioned the comparison of Spain and Portugal with England and Holland. Equally telling is the fact that nowhere did the industrial capitalism rise faster than in the United States – a society of free small owners (called farmers in the changed sense of this word) which was uniquely free from landlordism or any other form of 'primitive accumulation'. Significantly, the South – where there was plenty of 'primitive accumulation' in the form of slavery – played no part in this development. In the empire of the Tsars, southern Italy and Latin America 'primitive accumulation' was very intensive but its proceeds were squandered by the parasitic beneficiaries. And whereas it is true that there was considerable 'primitive accumulation' in England on the eve of the Industrial Revolution, the wealth acquired through piracy, the slave trade, extortion in India or even monopolistic trading under a royal charter, went into landed estates and gracious living around the court, while the new methods of production were financed from small profits and savings of master-craftsmen and small businessmen who could hardly be called 'capitalists', although this label fitted well enough many of their heirs by the time Marx was writing.

Perhaps under the undue influence of Marx, Weber usually talks about 'capitalism' where the term 'industrialism' (coined by Henri de Saint-Simon) would be more appropriate. Despite living about a half a century later, Marx failed to take into account the two factors which Saint-Simon emphatically pointed out as crucially distinctive of the modern world: the intellectual functions of invention (that is, research) and organisation. Indeed, on this point Marx's views fitted well enough France of the old regime, and perhaps even Prussia of his youth, but not at all England when he was living there. Stripped of their esoteric verbiage, the labour theory of value and the concept of 'surplus value' boil down to an assertion that only the manual workers really produce anything, while those who run the firms contribute nothing and therefore deserve to get nothing.

When the 'physiocrats' were describing the France of Louis the XV and XVI, they saw the idle nobility and the clergy, the unproductive officialdom and the army, supported by the work of the peasants who had to surrender a very substantial part of the wealth they produced without getting anything in return. So the physiocrats were not far from the truth in regarding the peasants as the sole productive class. Indeed, broadly speaking, the dichotomy between the producing and the ruling classes was a universal feature of all pre-industrial states. The unique feature of the industrial civilisation is that for the first time in history a large part – in recent times the majority – of the privileged class is involved in production albeit in the organising and directing capacity. Equally unique is the continuous shift in the importance of the contribution of the functions of organising, directing and inventing in comparison with purely manual labour. Saint-Simon clearly saw this – which was no mean feat at the beginning of the nineteenth century although it is obvious now.

Although Weber does not put it like this, and only once mentioned Saint-Simon (as far as I can recall), his thesis about the impact of Protestantism bears directly on this issue because it helps to explain the coupling of the privilege of wealth with the involvement in production. There is no mystery about why the poor work, as they do in all civilisations. But why should those who have more than enough for luxurious living go on working furiously? Why did Carnegie, Ford, Rockefeller, Edison and so many other businessmen and inventors, persist in their efforts when they could have relaxed and led a sybaritic existence? Perhaps they were very odd characters, but individual eccentricity cannot explain a mass phenomenon of millions of businessmen – not only self-made men but also many who had inherited wealth – who did not need to work for a living and yet went on working and saving. To invoke greed is no explanation because it does not answer the question of why should people be more acquisitive in certain epochs and countries than in others. In any case it is not true that the entrepreneurs who created the industrial capitalism were more acquisitive than the rich in other societies: one only has to think of the marriage arrangements among the landed nobility. It is true, on the other hand, that the pioneers of industrial capitalism were distinguished from the rich of other classes or cultures by their thrift and industriousness. Weber offers an explanation of this peculiarity, the validity of which we must now scrutinise.

5.3 Capitalism and the religions

Protestantism and catholicism

There are two kinds of argument in favour of Weber's thesis: one of them can be described as the argument from harmony; the other as the argument from co-variation. Let us look at them in turn. The argument from harmony consists in showing that capitalism can be developed only by people with certain characteristics, and that a given creed inculcates such traits.

It can be admitted as self-evident that capitalism cannot grow unless there are people who accumulate capital: that is to say, who do not spend everything they earn. The argument here is that Protestantism, and especially its Calvinist variety, taught thrift, whereas Catholicism did not. No religion, of course, has ever eradicated cupidity, but the disdain for material goods professed by the Catholic Church may have encouraged spending. Cupidity, after all, is something that comes naturally, whereas thrift is not. Thrift alone, however, is not enough.

An economic system whose propelling force is private accumulation of capital will not develop very fast if people are inclined to stop working as soon as they reach a certain level of affluence. Such a system can only progress if those who have already enough for their needs go on working and accumulating. The connection with Protestantism, particularly in its Calvinist variety, is that it taught people to regard work as a form of prayer, and the growth of possessions as evidence of the state of grace. Another important influence of Protestantism was its insistence on work as the only legitimate road to riches. Other religions, of course, also prohibit robbery and theft, but Protestant Puritanism is unique in condemning gambling. The religious ideals of work, thrift and enrichment without enjoyment and by means of work only, constitute what Weber calls 'worldly asceticism'. It is extremely plausible that a creed which preached this asceticism did in fact stimulate the growth of capitalism.

The argument that the Reformation first opened up possibilities of investment, by legitimising interest on loans, carried less force because in reality interest-taking was very common during the late Middle Ages, and by no means limited to parasitic usury. Nevertheless, it might be claimed that by removing the need for subterfuge, the Reformation helped to direct investment into productive channels, for clandestine gains are more readily linked with the parasitically exploitative than with the productive employment of capital. We can debate how much weight should be assigned to this factor, but the direction of its influence is beyond dispute.

The weakest point in the argument from harmony is the assertion linking the doctrine of predestination with the acquisitive drive. It is difficult to see how an earnest belief that one's fate is determined by something absolutely beyond one's control could stimulate anyone to exert himself. Fatalism (that is to say, belief in predestination) is generally considered to be one of the greatest obstacles to economic development in the Orient – an attitude which saps the spirit of enterprise as well as of workmanship. What seems to have happened is that the Protestants took the doctrine of predestination as little to heart as they did the old injunction to expose the other cheek to an assailant. It appears, therefore, that this tenet of Calvin's doctrine provided a stimulus to the growth of capitalism only in so far as it justified the unwillingness of the rich to share their wealth with the poor. This point is treated at greater length in my book *Syphilis, Puritanism and Witchcraft*, chapter 'Syphilis, Puritanism and Capitalism' (forthcoming).

The general conclusion which emerges from the foregoing analysis is that, although the doctrine of predestination constituted a neutral influence, worldly asceticism ought to have stimulated the growth of capitalism. In order to obtain further light on this thesis, let us look at the argument from co-variation.

The data included in Weber's essay as well as those supplied by later investigators show clearly that in countries and regions where the Protestants and the Catholics live intermingled, the former occupy a disproportionate number of prominent business positions. In France, for instance, Protestant influence in business is astonishing in view of the small numbers. In this case the explanation that their enthusiasm for business is due to being excluded from other fields of activity cannot be sustained because we would have to go right back to the *ancien régime* to find bars against the entry of Protestants into official posts. There remains a possibility that the mere fact of being in a minority has a bracing effect upon them, but the predominance of the Protestants over the Catholics in the economic life of a country like Germany, with a more or less evenly balanced population, cannot be accounted for in this way. Only in the cases of Ireland and Prussian Poland can the economic inferiority of the Catholics be possibly explained by the fetters imposed upon them by their Protestant rulers. For this reason these cases lend no support to Weber's thesis, but they do not contradict it either. It could be said that Protestant predominance in American business is due to the fact that they descend mainly from the old-established population, whereas the Catholics came more recently as poor immigrants, but for Canada and Holland this explanation plainly does not hold. The case of Holland is particularly significant because there the Catholics were a minority relegated to a politically subordinate position but with ample opportunities for business activities. In some ways their position resembled that of the Protestants in France after the end of legal discrimination. Nevertheless, they furnished far fewer successful businessmen than either the Protestants or the Jews. Thus, even if we allow for the influence of other factors, the data unambiguously suggest that Protestantism is more conducive to business activity than Catholicism.

We can adduce another argument from co-variation in support of Weber's thesis, using as our units of comparison states instead of sections of populations located within the boundaries of one state and pointing out that capitalism developed furthest and fastest in predominantly Protestant countries. In the world of today only the first part of this statement is true: the economies of English-speaking countries are no longer dominated by religious Protestants, and their rates of growth are exceeded by those of France, Italy, Western Germany, and above all Japan. The latter fact, however, does not invalidate the thesis of Weber, but only demands that we make explicit what is implicit: namely, that this thesis applies in full only to a situation where accumulation by private individuals constitutes the driving force of economic development. Once giant concerns and trusts enter upon the scene, and the 'ploughing back' of their undistributed profits becomes (jointly with state financing) the chief form of investment, worldly asceticism loses its importance because most of the saving then becomes in a sense 'forced'. It must be remembered, moreover, that Weber's analysis referred to an epoch when the margin of affluence was very much smaller than it is in the industrial countries of today, and as saving is more difficult for the less opulent, worldly asceticism sanctioned by

125

religion was necessary for the rapid accumulation and productive investment of capital. Another important qualification is that religious beliefs cannot affect economic behaviour decisively unless they are taken very seriously – not practised as a tranquillising make-believe, as commonly happens nowadays. The important point, which must be stressed again here, is that capitalist enterprise of non-predatory kind was developed by people who did not have very much money. There have always been large accumulations of liquid and real wealth in the hands of the economically parasitic individuals and corporations, but they contributed little to industrial growth, at least in its early stages. With the proviso, then, that it refers without qualifications only to economies consisting of small firms, the arguments from approximative co-variation support Weber's thesis. Nevertheless, owing to the bewildering complexity of this problem, these comparative data lend themselves to other interpretations as well.

In his *Materialistische Geschichtsauffassung* (by far the greatest work of comparative sociology produced by a Marxist) Karl Kautsky attempted to invert Weber's argument in accordance with the Marxist view that religion is a mere epiphenomenon without any causal efficacity – a view which is contradicted by Marx's statement that religion is the opium of the masses, for one cannot deny the power of opium. Narrating the spread of various heresies during the later Middle Ages, Kautsky (elaborating on Engels) shows how the class of artisans and petty businessmen provided a fertile ground for the conception and dissemination of ideas which found their final embodiment in Calvinism. For artisans and petty traders, fairly safe behind their walls from the depredations of feudal lords, hard work and saving were unique means of improving or even merely maintaining their positions. These conditions generated, according to Kautsky, the mentality which found its final sanction in Calvinism. This argument has considerable force: the evidence adduced by Kautsky and other writers does show that Calvinism struck roots above all in the cities where commerce and handicrafts prospered. The chief protagonists of Calvinism in German cities belonged to circles connected with business. Nevertheless, the thesis on the epiphenomenal character of Calvinism cannot be sustained because it fails to account for its spread among the Hungarian nobility and above all, for the conversion of Scotland. At the time of John Knox, the Scots, who later came to dominate English finance, were semi-tribal rustics famous for their dissolute habits. Knox and his followers made them into the most perfect examples of worldly asceticism. Here then the causation appears to have worked in the direction opposite to that suggested by Kautsky.

In Scotland Calvinism came to prevail without capitalism; in Italy capitalism failed to bring out religious schism of any kind. The case of Italy is particularly interesting because it contradicts not only Kautsky's thesis, but the extreme formulation of Weber's thesis as well: in Italy capitalism was born and prospered without any aid from Protestant ethic, and in fact the Papal See was one of the greatest centres of banking operations in the world. The Italians invented techniques so essential to capitalism as the bill of exchange and double-entry book-keeping, and they controlled banking in northern Europe until the seventeenth century: the main London street for headquarters of banks is still called Lombard Street. At the time of Calvin and John Knox capitalism was much more developed in Florence and Venice than in Geneva or Edinburgh. Presumably one of the reasons why Protestantism had so little appeal for the Italian bourgeoisie was the close connection of Italian bankers with the tributary machinery of the church – a fact which might have had something to do with the external manifestations of piety for which Florence (the seat of high finance) was renowned. The second reason might have been the Italians' disinclination to fight for their religious convictions: Machiavelli maintained that the nearer a place was to Rome the less truly pious were its inhabitants. Be that as it may, the fact remains that the example of Italy shows that neither Protestantism in general, nor Calvinism in particular can be regarded as mere epiphenomena of capitalism.

The thesis of Weber is affected only in the extreme formulations of some of its interpreters: for although the case of Italy proves that Calvinism could not have been a necessary condition of the emergence of capitalism, it does not rule out the possibility that Calvinism, had it been able to strike roots, could have given greater impetus to Italian capitalism. Indeed the evidence from Italy supports the less extreme interpretation of this thesis because Italian capitalism ceased to grow after the end of the sixteenth century, and indeed began to decline thereafter. The causes for this withering of economic growth are very difficult to unravel: there were a number of factors involved, such as the diminishing importance of the Mediterranean as a trade route, foreign invasions and wars between the Italian states, and so on. The spirit of enterprise had waned but as it had religious backing at no time, there is little reason to attribute this to the changes in religious outlook – religion may have had something to do with it but in an indirect way.

When we look at the geographical distribution of Catholic and

127

Protestant population, it seems so arbitrary that it is difficult to imagine that it could be the product of any such constant trend as the development of capitalism. A closer inspection of the process of the Reformation confirms this impression: a single battle often decided whether a country or a region was to remain Catholic or to become Protestant – and as is well known the outcomes of battles often depend on accidents. The princes' power of imposing the creed of their choice upon their subjects – proclaimed in the sinister principle of 'cuius regio eius religio' – enlarged the scope of chance, because actions of single individuals exhibit less regularity than the joint actions of large numbers.

Although in his writings on oriental religions Weber takes into account the indirect effects of religious beliefs, the explicit stress throughout his *Religionssoziologie* is on what he calls 'the economic ethic', that is to say, on the influence of the religious code of behaviour upon attitudes to business. But it might be argued that the influence of the ecclesiastical organisation upon the distribution of power was of greater consequence for the development of the economy. Some writers have argued that the most far-reaching impact of the Reformation consisted in replacing an autocratic ecclesiastic organisation by a looser one, thus weakening the conservative forces of society. Moreover, the Reformation furthered the growth of capitalism by effecting the confiscation of the gold possessed by the churches and monasteries, and putting it into circulation, thus eliminating the greatest source of thesaurisation which must have acted as a brake upon productive investment.

There is another way in which Protestantism may have stimulated the growth of capitalism. A perfectly capitalist society is not viable: when the sole motive of individual actions is the unbridled pursuit of gain, the administration of the state becomes disorderly and corrupt, and the growth of capitalism is therefore impeded. This is not a purely deductive argument because we can see that the countries where capitalism developed furthest and fastest, are blessed with more than average share of civic virtues. In the United States the great captains of industry may have been utterly ruthless and even dishonest, but on the whole the civic communal spirit was very strong there until very recently, and was much stronger when capitalism began to develop. England, Holland and lately Sweden have long been famous as examples (relative, of course) of orderliness and civic virtues, and for their adherence to the principle that honesty is the best policy. The same can be said about the Germans, in spite of their authoritarian proclivities. The case of Japan also shows how civic virtues are useful to capitalism, but this case is irrelevant when comparing Catholicism with Protestantism. It must be noted, on the other hand, that all the so-called under-developed countries are conspicuous for their lack of public spirit and of honesty in commercial dealings. Is this the cause of their poverty or the consequences? Weber's thesis suggests that it is a cause.

If we accept as valid the assumption that capitalism requires a good measure of civic virtues if it is to prosper, we face the question of whether this has anything to do with Protestantism, and if so whether it is not entirely a matter of circular causation: for it might be argued that widespread poverty undermines civic virtues while the lack of them makes poverty difficult to eliminate. It is a fact, however, that if we compare Protestant with Catholic countries, the difference in the prevalence of civic virtues is striking. Without going into the intricacies of the possible causes, we must note the possibility that Protestantism might have stimulated the growth of capitalism indirectly, by fostering the civic virtues required for the smooth functioning of the state. The contention that Protestantism stimulated the growth of capitalism in indirect ways which cannot be subsumed under Weber's concept of economic ethic, far from disproving Weber's thesis merely amplifies it. We shall come back to this question in the next chapter.

Some weight must be assigned to the complete lack of arguments in favour of the contrary thesis that Catholicism is or was more propitious than Protestantism, to the development of capitalism. At most it might be argued that under certain circumstances Calvinism fails to produce much spirit of capitalist enterprise. Among the examples which might be cited to this point the most conspicuous are the Calvinist Hungarian nobility and the Boers of South Africa – although the Boers do show somewhat more inclination towards 'worldly asceticism' and business activity than the people in economically analogous positions in Catholic countries. On the whole, then, if we bear in mind that Weber claimed that Protestantism fostered the development of capitalism, but nowhere said that it was its sole cause, we can accept his thesis as valid.

Judaism

The volume of *Religionssoziologie* devoted to Judaism is unquestioningly a great work, full of illuminating insights and brilliant suggestions; nevertheless, its central theme sheds little light on the relation between religion and the rise of capitalism, simply because as an economic force Judaism was unimportant, as Jews were a very small nation, leading a precarious interstitial existence, oppressed and pushed around by mighty nations and empires. As far as the evolution of ancient capitalism was concerned, the nature of their religion was of no consequence: no matter how conducive to capitalist activity it might have been, the shaping of the economy (even of their own little country) was not in their hands.

During the earlier parts of the Middle Ages the primitive condition of society ruled out any development of capitalism. As soon as it became materially possible, the Jews began to play a prominent role in commerce and banking but, as they were under residential restrictions and not allowed to own land, they were not in a position to take part in the development of industry.

As soon as the restrictions imposed upon them ceased to be crippling, the Jews proved to be at least as successful in business as the Calvinists, but by then capitalism was already fully developed. Since the successful Jewish businessmen were as a rule just as pious as their Calvinist counterparts, there is no reason to think that the economic ethic of Judaism is in any way less propitious to capitalist activity than Calvinism. Indeed it would be strange if it were so, because the teachings of Protestantism (particularly of its Puritanical varieties) consisted mainly of the precepts of ancient Judaism.

Weber believed that the Jews could not have become the principal promoters of the nascent capitalism because they were incapacitated for this role by their 'double ethics' which made their commercial transactions insufficiently predictable. It is clear, however, that this bias does not belong to the core of Judaism and is perfectly explicable as a response to persecution and disdain. Where the Jews were not harassed and achieved opulence, they usually conducted business just as respectably as anybody else. None the less, an industrial revolution could not have been led by a segregated and fettered religious minority.

In his famous book *The Jews and Modern Capitalism*, Werner Sombart argued that the Jews were the true creators of capitalism. He based his contention on a number of instances in which an arrival of Jews in substantial numbers was followed by an efflorescence of business activity and a rapid growth of wealth. This was the case with Holland, Venice, the city of Frankfurt and many others. Contrariwise, expulsions of the Jews were in several instances followed by the economic decline of a city or even a whole country, as was the case with Spain. However, Sombart does not take into account the data which do not fit his thesis, such as the fact that in England the foundations of capitalism were laid during the period between the expulsion of the Jews and their return. It could even be argued that the presence of a very large number of Jews was fatal to the development of capitalism as the Jews were much more numerous in the economically backward eastern Europe than in the countries with a developed capitalist system. The causation here is extremely involved.

Originally it was the economic backwardness which caused the influx of the Jews in eastern Europe: objects of animosity from their gentile competitors in more highly urbanised lands in western Europe, they were welcomed in countries without a native trading class. However, their presence in large numbers acted subsequently as a brake upon commercial development because as soon as trade came to be monopolised by the Jews it became a depressed occupation. Being isolated from the surrounding population, the Jews were in a much weaker position than the bourgeoisie integrated with the rest of the society, and therefore they were unable to resist the encroachments of the nobility; which was the reason why the Polish and Hungarian nobles preferred them.

In spite of the startling achievements of its adherents in the field of business, Judaism could never become a decisive factor in the development of capitalism because it was a religion of a minority of strangers which could never mould the character of any European nation. The Jews neither wished nor had the chance to convert to their faith the Christian majority; and it was out of the question that they should attain a truly dominating position in any country of the diaspora. In consequence, the Jews could use their aptitude for capitalist enterprise when the circumstances were propitious but were powerless to create them.

Weber was partly right: Judaism was not a crucial factor in the rise of capitalism; but he was wrong in imputing this to its economic ethic. This ethic was extremely favourable to capitalism but its influence was always severely limited by the exclusivist character of Judaism.

Confucianism

Weber's volume on China constitutes an even greater contribution to sociology than his volume on Judaism, but nevertheless its general thesis is wrong, as in part we have already seen. True, everything influences everything in social life, and there can be little doubt that by contributing in some way to the maintenance of the structure of traditional Chinese society, Confucianism somehow acted as an indirect brake upon the development of capitalism; but as far as the direct influence *via* economic ethic is concerned, it does not appear that Confucianism impeded capitalist activity in any way. Analysing this problem along lines similar to the foregoing treatment of Protestantism above, let us first examine the argument from harmony – or rather disharmony.

In spite of what Weber says, I think that it is difficult to find among the tenets of Confucianism anything directly opposed to capitalist activity. Filial piety, patriarchalism and family solidarity do not hamper business very much, and were by no means absent from European civilisation at the time of the rise of capitalism. Ritualism (which is the factor stressed by Weber) was, it is true, very marked in traditional China, but it concerned personal relations – not economic activities. The general outlook of Confucianism was practical and rationalist. As we saw earlier, Weber was wrong in maintaining that Christianity contributed to the 'demagicalisation' (*Entzauberung*) of the view of the world whereas Confucianism in fact did. An early critic of Weber describes Confucianism as 'worldly, economically oriented and rationalist. A more propitious ground for economic development is hardly conceivable' (Arthur von Rosthorn, 'Religion und Wirtschaft in China', in vol. 2 of *Erinnerungsgabe für Max Weber*, ed. Melchior Palyi, Munich, 1923).

The fact that Confucianist literature assigned a low status to merchants cannot be regarded as an important factor for two reasons: firstly, because it was not uncommon in the ideological literature of the countries where capitalism was rising; and secondly, because it was an effect rather than a determining factor of the existing distribution of power, as can be seen from the fact that the equally low status assigned to soldiers in Confucianist writings did not prevent them from attaining very high positions, and at times dominating the society.

Although many of its preconditions – such as well-developed transport and currency, a wide area of peaceful commerce, and a very high level of handicrafts – existed in China, capitalist industry could not develop there because of the fetters imposed upon business enterprise by the bureaucratic state. Officials always regarded businessmen with resentment and employed many means to keep them down. Fiscal extortion prevented, if not accumulation of profits, at least their regular investment in productive establishments which was in any case difficult owing to the official regulation of location and methods of production. That these factors, and not economic ethic, were responsible for the arrest of capitalism in traditional China is demonstrated by the business drive of the Chinese emigrants to British and Dutch colonies, most of whom continued to adhere strictly to their traditional religion: within the institutional framework of these colonies, their religion did not impede capitalist enterprise, in which the Chinese immigrants were phenomenally successful. More recently, the compatibility of the Chinese traditional values with capitalist enterprise has been amply demonstrated in Hong Kong, Singapore and Taiwan.

Confucianism, then, did constitute a serious obstacle to the development of capitalism, but it did so not through the influence of its economic ethic upon the behaviour of those engaged in commerce and industry but in virtue of its fitness to serve as a political formula cementing the bureaucratic state.

Hinduism

The central theme of Weber's volume on Hinduism is less open to criticism because Hinduism did constitute a formidable obstacle to the rise of capitalism, owing to its numerous taboos prohibiting utilisation of resources, and impeding collaboration in production by enjoining avoidance between persons of different castes. Although parasitic capitalism based on usury had flourished in India since time immemorial (as Weber was the first to show), the capitalist mode of production together with large-scale trade was first introduced by the British, and began to strike root as a native growth only when the hold of Hinduism became less astringent, owing to the spread of laicism.

The esoteric mysticism of the Brahmins had, no doubt, something to do with the withering of the early buds of Hindu science, but as far as the shaping of the economy was concerned, more important was the support which Hinduism lent to social parasitism by making the toiling masses listless and utterly servile. As Weber rightly pointed out, with its promise of reincarnation into a higher caste as the reward for keeping dutifully to one's station in life, Hinduism functioned as the most powerful 'opium of the people' ever invented, which fortified parasitism and the ruthless fiscal extortion which diverted energies and wealth from production.

The ritual barriers dividing them from one another, together with the addiction to self-mortification, made it difficult for the Hindus to defend themselves against invasions, each wave of which aggravated insecurity and exploitation. Moreover, since the division of labour was dove-tailed with the caste barriers sanctified by the religion, the methods of production tended towards a ritualistic petrifaction, as Weber correctly noted. So, his thesis stands: Hinduism was effective in preventing the rise of capitalism in India, not only indirectly *via* its influence on the structure of power, but also directly *via* its economic ethic.

133

5.4 Ethics and economics

Distracted (as in so many other places) by the confusing notion of rationalisation, Weber is not entirely consistent in what he says about the link between the ethic and business enterprise: in *The Protestant Ethic and the Spirit of Capitalism* he talks about stimulation of the desire for profit as an important aspect of the new religion, whereas in his works on the Asiatic and Ancient civilisations he repeatedly states that greed for money is a common characteristic in no way peculiar to modern capitalism. He thus contradicts himself as it is difficult to imagine a greedy trader not wanting to make profit. Anyone who has bought anything on an oriental market knows that the traders there are at least as eager to maximise their profits as any Western businessman. Furthermore, a one-time colleague and sympathetic critic of Weber, Lujo Brentano, has convincingly shown in an article 'Puritanismus und Kapitalismus' (reprinted in a book *Der Wirtschaftende Mensch in die Geschichte*, Leipzig, 1923) that the Puritans disapproved of greed and unbridled profit-making no less than did the Catholic theologians. Brentano backs his argument by quoting the parts of Weber's sources which the latter left unquoted. In view of this it seems best to disregard Weber's self-contradiction and to follow him when he says that the desire for profit is too common to be regarded as responsible for the commercial and industrial progress of the West.

The legitimation of interest-taking was Calvin's innovation, but its importance lay not in the fact that it stimulated this activity, extensively practised long before the Reformation not only by the laity but also by bishops, monasteries and the popes. Actually, the legitimation reduced usury in the sense of charging high rates. As Henri Hauser says, 'the Calvinist societies, where usury was allowed, become very soon societies where money cost less than where usury was prohibited. . . . This explains the development of investment in countries like Holland and Geneva' (Henri Hauser, *Les Idées Economiques de Calvin in Les Débuts du Capitalisme*, Paris, 1931). By permitting the practice for which there was much demand the law became less exposed to 'being circumvented or broken. This, however, was only a small part of the fundamental change wrought by Protestantism: namely, a general enhancement of honesty and respect for the law. Albeit he gets it mixed up with an advance of rationality (disregarding the obvious fact that cheating can be perfectly rational if it is successful), Weber is aware of the importance of honesty to economic progress as can be seen from his statement that the Jews could not have developed 'rational capitalism' because of their 'double ethics' which allowed them to cheat the unbelievers. Although, as I have pointed out earlier, the Jews were in no position to transform the economic system no matter what their beliefs might have been, Weber is right in thinking that customs which permit cheating constitute an obstacle to the development of commerce. He was wrong, however, in seeing the Jewish 'double ethics' as something peculiar because cheating is well-nigh universal in the primitive forms of trade between strangers, especially when they differ in culture or religion. Not merely cheating but also robbery commonly accompanied trade. The Vikings, for instance, after they finished trading, would often change their trade flag for a war flag and take back by force what they have sold – a practice likely to reduce the volume of trade.

Economic development has built-in deterrents against the most short-sighted kinds of crookery and robbery but we have plenty of evidence from our own times that the level of honesty and respect for the law may decline rather than rise in step with economic growth. It follows that it must be treated as an (at least partially) independent variable. The spirit of enterprise often overflows the legal and moral embankments. Although people often drift into crime under the promptings of laziness, big gangsters and crooks show plenty of initiative and work very hard. The choice between honest and dishonest dealing does not depend only on a rational calculation of likely gains and losses, but also on the prevalent moral attitudes which largely stem from the religion. And it is not just the matter of how business transactions are conducted but also of the behaviour of the agents of the state. When the rulers grab whatever they can, the judges, officials and policemen accept or extort bribes, business trans-actions are not only less predictable but also mixed with conspiracy and coercion. Though disregarded by our experts on economic development and planning, it is an old discovery that honest politics and administration are essential conditions of economic progress. This is so today and was no less true at the dawn of capitalism.

Venality is very difficult to eradicate because it is often spread by those whose duty is to prevent it. Many examples show that even the most atrocious punishments have little effect. One of the caliphs, for instance, began to punish bribe-takers and embezzlers by skinning them alive and making their successors sit on cushions made with the skins of the culprits. Yet even this did not stop the new satraps from doing the same because they had to get money to bribe the courtiers, failing which they would be falsely accused and condemned. The functioning of the economy and the state depends also on the honesty and the sense of duty

135

of the ordinary people but these can be moulded by regular application of appropriate punishments and rewards. Regularity in this matter, however, can be maintained only if the rulers act in accordance with the proclaimed principles. The nearer to the top a person is, the more important is his self-discipline.

Bemused by his notion of rationalisation, Weber did not realise that he was right in bringing an ideational factor into an explanation of economic progress precisely because the required attitudes (honesty, the sense of duty and dedication to work) do not stem from a rational pursuit of self-interest but have the nature of categorical imperatives, to use Kant's famous term. The moral principles are, of course, products of socio-cultural processes, but the causation here is more complex and mysterious than a market mechanism. Though in need of elucidation, Weber's insight into the link between ethic and economy constitutes a contribution of enduring value which must be taken into account not only in explaining the past but also in understanding the present.

It is worth noting in passing that this viewpoint is missing in most debates about the relative virtues of collectivism versus the market. True, the protagonists of the latter sometimes use the argument that corruption nullifies any advantages which central planning might have, but they fail to recognise the influence of moral standards on the functioning of a market economy. This is not surprising because if they did recognise it they would have to admit the limitations of self-interest as a sufficient cement of society. Like the Marxists, the followers of Hayek and Milton Friedman believe that one remedy can cure all the ills: the sanctity of private property and freedom of the market play in their doctrine a part which is analogous to that of collectivisation and central planning in Marxism. To appreciate how simple-minded are both these doctrines, think of medicine and imagine two schools: one advocating plenty of food, the other plenty of exercise, as the infallible and only road to good health. It is also worth noting that there is an inconsistency in the propaganda of doctrinaire free-marketeers: they postulate that the desire for profit is invariably laudable and the only reliable motive on which a society can rest, and yet they criticise the groups – especially the unions – who use political influence to obtain a larger share of wealth. Why should anybody renounce the use of power to make a gain, if there are no moral considerations which can override the quest for profit? After these asides, let us go back to the question of the historical impact of Protestantism.

One of the necessary conditions of industrial progress was elimination of despotism, that is a curtailment of the power of the monarchs and their servants. Productive investment became worthwhile only when nobody had the power to grab other people's possessions at will. Constitutional limitations on the use of power, the rule of law and elected assemblies – which together can be subsumed under the concept of constitutionalism – were the cornerstones of the type of polity which made property secure from seizure. The Reformation fostered evolution in this direction. Even Lutheranism and Anglicanism have contribued to this effect, despite their politically subservient character, simply by shaking the monolithic structure of the Church. With the Puritan churches there is a clear consonance between their democratic organisation and the representative institutions in the state. Although Calvin set up in Geneva one of the most oppressive theocracies in history, the content of his teachings steadily undermined the principle of hierarchy. The first democratic polities came into existence under the influence of Calvinism in Switzerland and the United States, the latter branching off from the parliamentary tradition of Protestant Britain. Only in one other pre-industrial country did the parliament acquire supremacy: in the kingdom of Poland and Lithuania which sank into anarchy and was finally dismembered at the end of the eighteenth century. This end was largely due to the character of the Polish parliament as the organ of the land-owning nobility, while the townsmen were relatively few, poor, mostly alien (namely Jews), and without political rights. The respect for the law, characteristic of the Protestant countries was entirely lacking.

The Protestant respect for the law, which permitted the development of representative government in some countries, made the authoritarian states more efficient. The best example is Prussia. The orderliness, industriousness, cleanliness and discipline of the Prussians were the fruits of the conjunction of the Lutheranism of the subjects with the Calvinism of the ruling dynasty: while the first furthered dutiful obedience, the second fostered self-discipline and dedication to the impersonal ideal (or idol, if you like) of the state. In contrast to Louis XIV's famous utterance 'l'état c'est moi', Frederick II of Prussia kept saying that he was the first servant of the state. He made widely known the incidents which ended by his rewarding an underling who forced him to obey his own decree, as in the case of a guardsman who did not let him enter some place because this was against regulations. This concern for giving his subjects a good example of law-abidingness did not prevent him from being a very harsh taskmaster. In comparison with the extravagant self-indulgence and profligacy of other dynasties, the Hohenzollerns appear as ascetic, thrifty and dedicated drill-masters who succeeded in moulding their subjects into excellent soldiers and workers. It seems that their conversion to Calvinism in the seventeenth century was a crucial turn in the evolution of the Prussian mentality.

It seems that the stricter observance of the legal and moral rules among the Protestants stemmed from their elevation of the scriptures to the status of the sole source of knowledge of good and evil, which entailed a diminution of the role of the priests. It is completely misleading to call this change 'rationalisation', because it is in no way more rational to believe something just because it is written rather than spoken. Nevertheless, there is a big difference between doing what one is told by a priest and being guided by a book which has been written long ago and cannot be changed. The latter attitude precludes (instead of entailing) a mental submission to another man who can change the tenets and the rules of conduct to suit his convenience.

The second circumstance, which increased the congruence between the ethic and the behaviour among the Protestants, was the abolition of confessions followed by an absolution, which made it easy to erase guilt and start sinning again with a clean slate. Having to live with the burden of guilt appears to have made the Protestants less cheerful and sociable, but (through the operation of mental mecahnisms brought to light by Freud) it made them more eager to punish and stamp out transgressions.

While making its consequences more painful, the Reformation made it easier to avoid sin by eliminating the rules which only a few saints could consistently follow. By far the most important step in this direction was the abolition of celibacy of the clergy. The spectacle of the moral mentors doing the opposite of what they preached encouraged a disrespect for all rules among the Catholics. Hardly less important was economic permissiveness which legitimised what was going on in defiance of the teachings of the church. The latter condemned not only the charging of interest and making profits beyond what was needed for decent living, but any accumulation of wealth. Private property was treated as a regrettable though unavoidable concession to the weakness of human nature until 1891 when Leo XIII declared it to be good. None the less, not only the church as an institution or the monasteries but even individual bishops, not to speak of the popes, amassed vast riches, this giving a contagious example of disregard for the professed principles. Although rule-breaking is a ubiquitous feature of social life, the divergence between the norms and the behaviour among the Protestants appears to have been generally less extreme. The greater congruence in this respect has helped the growth of industry and trade in two ways: directly, by raising the levels of honesty and reliability in economic activities; and indirectly by aiding the development of the type of state which respects the rights of the citizen, including the rights of property, and functions in accordance with rules. To this was added the stimulus to saving and investment provided by the high valuation of work combined with the abhorrence of laziness and self-indulgence.

Max Weber was very right in looking for a religious factor of economic change but chains of causes and effects have no ends. As I have tried to show elsewhere, the change in religious attitudes was influenced by a medical factor: namely the epidemic of syphilis.

5.5   The position of cities and the military factor

Although he makes no brief general statement to this effect, it is perfectly clear from everything he says that Weber regards the position of the cities as the key factor in the development of capitalism and therefore of the other distinctive features of the occidental civilisation. However, I must underline the word '*position*' because it would have been no discovery to say at the end of the nineteenth century that development of the economy (or of capitalism or the civilisation in general) depended on or involved the growth of the cities. The originality of Weber lies in his ideas about the determining factors and the consequence of the cities' position in the power structure of the state.

In the light of the much more extensive and reliable data which we have today we can see how right Weber was in seeking the key to an explanation of the rise of capitalism in the position of the cities rather than their sheer size. In 1600 the eleven largest cities in the world were to be found not in western Europe – where 'the spirit of capitalism' was rising and was being reinforced by the Reformation – but in China, the Ottoman empire, India of the Moguls and Japan. Tertius Chandler and Gerald Fox (in *3000 years of Urban Growth*, New York, 1974) give the following figures (in thousands): Peking 706, Istanbul 700, Agra 500, Cairo 400 Osaka 400, Canton 350, Yedo 350, Kyoto 350, Hangchow 350, Lahore 350, Nanking 317. The largest city in Europe was Naples (275), which was certainly not in the forefront of progress. The places which at that time were leading in the development of capitalism were relatively small: Florence 65, Genoa 70, Amsterdam 48, Augsburg 48, Lübeck 31. Among the commercial cities only London (187) and Venice (151) were

139

relatively large; but their size was partly due to their function as political capitals.

Synthesising what Weber says about the cities in his various works, we can distil a thesis which (like all good theories) is simple in its fundamental idea, but raises many complicated questions. It is that the more advanced capitalist forms of production and exchange can develop only where the cities are dominated by the mercantile class (rather than bureaucrats, priests or soldiers), and where they are strong enough to win autonomy, but not so strong as to be able to live by exploiting the rural population or by imperialism. This theory is not incompatible with Weber's thesis about the impact of Protestantism, which can be regarded as having provided an additional stimulus to accumulation of capital in a situation where the aforementioned conditions were present.

As ancient Greece and Rome were very different from Western Christendom, we may ask whether Weber was right in following the usage common among historians when he spoke of the Occident as a cultural entity different from the rest of Eurasia, including Byzantium and Muscovy. In other words, are there any traits of social structure or culture which Greece and Rome had in common with the Western Christendom but which were absent in the rest of the world? In my opinion it is legitimate to construe such a cultural entity because the Occident in this sense had the following unique features. First, it has produced political systems with legal (as distinguished from merely practical) limitations on royal power. The ultimate stage of this tendency was a complete elimination of monarchic power and emergence of government by elected office-holders and assemblies. Government by assembly was common enough in small tribes throughout the world but only in the Occident has it appeared in states. To be exact, small republics have existed for a short time in ancient India but they were soon absorbed into the Mauryan empire and left no cultural heritage. The precondition of its distinctive evolution was another peculiarity of the Occident which consisted of the absence of divine kingship which was the lynch-pin of oriental despotism. The absence of despotism in the Occident was only relative because the late Roman empire, some of the conquest states in the early Middle Ages and some of the absolutist states in the eighteenth century came quite near to it. It is also true that until the recent times juridical defence was vouchsafed in only a meagre measure to the lower classes. None the less, the experience of living under authority bridled by entrenched rights, elections and deliberative assemblies, left such deep traces, and was so closely connected with other unique traits, that we can treat the peoples marked by this experience as forming a cultural entity which merits a name.

To the list of unique features of the Occident Weber adds the autonomy and internal cohesion of the city. And in his rather disjointed but marvellously insightful way he inquires into the circumstances which have permitted this configuration to emerge. Among these he attributes an important role to customs and beliefs which facilitate or impede a political union of the city-dwellers. He thinks that the caste in India, the solidarity of the clan in China and various ritual barriers in the Near East forestalled the possibility of fraternisation and conjuration of the burghers which in the medieval Occident were the first steps in their fight for autonomy. He also thinks that the church's encouragement of communal ceremonies followed by festivities, prepared the ground for the fraternisation of the citizenry, in contrast to Hinduism where all the rites and feasts take place within the caste. On the other side of the balance, anything which fosters bureaucracy and despotism makes it more difficult for the cities to win autonomy. One of such factors is dependence of agriculture on massive works of irrigation. On this point Weber elaborates on Marx and anticipates Wittfogel, without going to the latter's extreme of seeing in it the ubiquitous root of all despotism. In contrast, dependence on foreign trade (as in ancient Greece or medieval Italy) makes centralised control over resources more difficult and therefore fosters a dispersion of political power.

Weber's explanation of the non-emergence of capitalism in Asia is, so to speak, overdetermined as he indicates more than one sufficient condition. What he says about the structure of the state (i.e. bureaucratic despotism), as well as about the lack of autonomy of the cities and the consequent subjection of the merchants and artisans, suffices to explain the absence of economic progress along capitalist lines, which he also attributes to the peculiarities of the economic ethic moulded by religion. As we saw earlier, the latter explanation has a much more limited validity.

Reading his interpretation of the evolution of Greek and Roman societies, we can see that the autonomy of the cities can only be a necessary but not a sufficient condition of development of new forms of production and trade, because in the ancient Graeco-Roman civilisation the cities were not only independent but dominant, and yet capitalism developed only within fairly narrow limits, then stagnated and eventually withered. Weber's explanation of the arrest and decline of the ancient capitalism rests upon his distinction between unproductive or parasitic capitalism (which he calls 'irrational') and productively or industrially oriented capitalism (which he calls 'rational'). Although he does not say it explicitly, his explanation also rests upon the tacit but correct premise that only the latter is capable of self-sustained growth whereas the former tends towards self-strangulation because at best it only transfers wealth and usually destroys it. The capitalism of antiquity failed to develop new methods of production because it oriented itself towards the extraction of wealth from the conquered populations. Instead of being dominated by producers and traders the ancient city became, as Weber vividly puts it, a warriors' guild. Why did this occur in the antiquity but not in the Middle Ages?

To explain this, Weber points to the difference in the techniques of warfare: in antiquity the infantry, which could be concentrated in towns, was the strongest arm whereas in the Middle Ages the battlefields were dominated by the cavalry which had to be dispersed throughout the countryside where there was fodder. The armed medieval townsmen could defend their walls but were incapable of subjugating the rural populations where the horse-riding nobility remained the ruling class. On the other hand, the dispersion of political power, connected with the rudimentary condition of the administrative machinery, permitted the cities to win rights which protected them from oppression and exploitation and enabled their inhabitants to retain the fruits of their labours and innovations.

As thus distilled from Weber's dispersed explanations of particular cases, a simple general thesis may be restated as follows: new forms of production and trade (i.e. industrially oriented capitalism) develop only where the business class is too strong to be fettered and exploited but not strong enough to accumulate wealth by extracting it from others, and where, in consequence, production and trade offer to the members of this class the most promising road to satisfactory livelihood or enrichment. This thesis is of great explanatory power and offers the key to the understanding of many cases with which Weber did not deal. I have used it in my studies of Africa and Latin America and hope to show further examples of its fruitfulness in forthcoming works.

The distinction between productive (i.e. industrial or 'rational') and parasitic (i.e. political or 'irrational') capitalism is related to another which Weber stresses: namely, between producers' and consumers' cities. It was an aspect of the normal human pattern that cities were centres of exploitation and consumption rather production. The small but largely independent cities of Western Christendom during the later Middle Ages were the first to be populated mainly by producers (if we include the traders) and to give to the producers juridical security, a high status and a share in the government. The foregoing twinned distinctions constitute Weber's most important conceptual innovation, as they offer a key to the complex of ideas which explain why Western civilisation departed from the normal human pattern.

The foregoing account should help to demonstrate the benefits which can be obtained from Weber if his works are approached in the spirit of critical but constructive analysis. They are a marvellous store of illuminating ideas presented mostly in a rough-hewn and often opaque form. Like every other mortal, he was sometimes mistaken but only some of his classificatory efforts can be regarded as of little value. His causal explanations always raise interesting questions; and even if inadequate or wrong, constitute a useful opening for a more systematic inquiry. The most rewarding approach, I think, is to search for tacit general premises of his explanations of various turns of social evolution, to attempt to formulate them clearly and to confront them with data which were unknown in his time.

6 Conclusion: what should we learn from Weber to advance farther?

To answer this question I must begin by repeating what I have said in the Foreword as well as in other publications about other great writers of the past: neither ancestor worship nor patricide permits progress. Understanding cannot advance without constant sifting of the stock of knowledge and the fitting together of the bits which have passed scrutiny with ideas which are genuinely new in content rather than merely new labels. Moreover, to appreciate the merits of a thinker we must not confuse a disqualifying mistake with one which might have been inevitable given the state of knowledge, and which either has provided or might provide a starting point for fruitful inquiries by others. Columbus was a great discoverer although he did not know which continent he had discovered, but any navigator who repeated his mistake fifty years later would have been disqualified. Likewise, Auguste Comte and Karl Marx had various erroneous notions, which they had created and which were mostly excusable at the time and perhaps a necessary price of their inventiveness: who ventures on new paths is likely to take a wrong turning here and there. These mistakes do not justify denying them the title to greatness, although they disqualify as a serious scholar anyone who clings to them now. The same applies to Weber, although his misconceptions appear to us as less gross because the difference in the amount of accumulated knowledge between his time and ours is much less.

We ought to be inspired by Weber's titanic efforts but we shall not get further by imitating slavishly his way of working or expressing himself. Just as no one can emulate the achievement of the early anthropologists who revealed to the reading public strikingly different cultures, so you could not repeat Weber's feat of an almost single-handed exploration of a great civilisation mainly from primary sources because these have by now been digested by a crowd of specialists. Anyone writing today who disregarded the large sinological literature and tried to rely mainly on his own study of translated primary sources would produce something as far off the mark as Amerigo Vespucci's map of the coast of America. Perhaps the correctness of Weber's picture of China is no greater but in 1920 there was nothing better or even like it. Now there are no civilisations to be surveyed single-handedly just as there are no islands to be mapped.

Analogous considerations apply to comparative analysis: in some ways it became easier because much more information about social structures is available in secondary sources. It is even possible to make a contribution in this field relying only on the literature in English. Weber astonishes us because to a large extent he was using in his comparative arguments and surveys the factual information which he culled from primary sources. Nowadays it would amount to a misallocation of effort to do the same because the time put by a comparatist into studying primary sources would be better spent on reading secondary literature. Given that so much time and effort has been invested in various areas, periods and aspects by the specialists, it is unlikely that somebody who can only dabble with primary sources would come up with new facts. The only thing which a comparatist can do in the present state of knowledge is to try to discover connections between facts which the area specialists cannot see precisely because their focus is narrow and they do not compare their case with similar and contrasting cases. A practical lesson follows from this: there is little to be gained by backing up a theory derived from comparative analysis by case studies as bulky as Weber's volumes of *Religionssoziologie*, as there is no point in offering a general picture drawn by a relative amateur when very full pictures by specialists are available. Furthermore, since there is so much more to read than in Weber's time, brevity is much more important than it was then; and for this reason alone not more factual evidence ought to be cited in support of a theoretical proposition than is needed to prove the point.

Since he does not need to spend so much time burrowing in primary sources, a comparatist of today ought to pay more attention to the logical structure of the argument, and to attain a higher degree of clarity and precision than Weber did. He was so full of ideas and in such a hurry to gather factual information to back them that he never formulated his theses carefully, never examined or weighed up arguments for and against, never made clear what were his premises or implications. Nor does he ever

145

grade his assertions by the degree of likelihood: expressions like 'might be', 'likely', 'it seems', 'perhaps', are difficult to find in his writings. He ploughs through mounds of factual information and churns up a flood of rough rule-of-the-thumb generalisations, explanations and suggestive comparisons. Like the early explorers of unknown continents, he does not bother about exactitude because he is in a hurry as there is so much that has never been mapped, and the first sketch must be rough. Today, however, if anyone wants to build on Weber's contributions and get beyond them, he must attain a greater degree of order and precision. The question is: how much greater?

It seems that to every stage in the development of a science corresponds a broadly circumscribed optimum of exactitude. Some historians of physics say that if Copernicus or Kepler had much more exact measurements of the movements of celestial bodies at their disposal, they might have lost faith in their theories, refrained from putting them forth and science might never have developed. Logical difficulties about the concepts of differential and integral calculus were not resolved until the nineteenth century, and Berkeley's proof that it was self-contradictory was logically correct. If Newton had given more weight to philosophical precision than to the fact that the 'fluxions' (as he called calculus) 'worked' (in the sense of enabling him to make true predictions) he might have abandoned his theories. He might also have done it had he known about the divergence of the planets' orbits from what followed from his theorems. A somewhat similar relationship beween precision and the stage of development (whether in exactitude or measurement or in logical rigour) appears to exist in the social sciences where, of course, the degree of imprecision and the likelihood of complete error are of an altogether different order. So, although we must improve on Weber on these points if we want to go beyond him, we must take care not to overshoot the mark.

Methodology must be the guiding light but trying to grasp the unattainable – like emulating the exactitude of physics – is a sure recipe for sterility. Weber's methodological nonchalance – strange in a writer who made important contributions to this subject – shows how far an inquirer can get despite the lack of method, provided he has a powerful intelligence and imagination and a wide knowledge of the facts. So, although greater logical order and clarity can be expected today than in Weber's time, moderation is desirable even in the pursuit of methodological rigour which is worthless if achieved by moving on the level of abstractions disconnected from reality. And this brings us to the final and most important lesson which we can learn from Weber:

namely that comparative study of history (including, of course, very recent history) must remain the main method of substantiating any theory which claims to explain large-scale social processes.

Index

148

Printed in the USA/Agawam, MA
December 1, 2010

555338.094